D1158352

Management Wisdom
— *from the* —
New York Yankees'
Dynasty

Management Wisdom

from the

New York Yankees' Dynasty

What Every Manager Can Learn from a Legendary Team's 80-Year Winning Streak

Lance A. Berger
with Dorothy R. Berger

WILEY

John Wiley & Sons, Inc.

Published by John Wiley & Sons, Inc., Hoboken, New Jersey.
Published simultaneously in Canada.

For general information on our other products and services please contact our Customer Care Department within the United States at (800) 762-2974, outside the United States at (317) 572-3993 or fax (317) 572-4002.

Wiley also publishes its books in a variety of electronic formats. Some content that appears in print may not be available in electronic books. For more information about Wiley products, visit our web site at www.Wiley.com.

Library of Congress Cataloging-in-Publication Data:
Berger, Lance A.
    Management wisdom from the New York Yankees dynasty : what every manager can learn from a legendary team's 80-year winning streak / Lance A. Berger and Dorothy R. Berger.
        p.   cm.
"Published simultaneously in Canada."
ISBN-13 978-0-471-71554-2 (cloth : alk. paper)
ISBN-10 0-471-71554-9 (cloth : alk. paper)
    1. Management.   2. Organizational effectiveness.   3. New York Yankees (Baseball team)—Management.   I. Berger, Dorothy R.   II. Title.
HD31.B397 2005
796.357'64'0683—dc22

                                                                    2005001065

Printed in the United States of America.

10   9   8   7   6   5   4   3   2   1

Contents

Acknowledgments

We would like to recognize Andrew Littell, fervent Yankee fan and writer, who enthusiastically championed the concept for this book. Special thanks to Richard Narramore, Senior Editor at John Wiley & Sons, who helped bring this project to fruition.

We also acknowledge the contributions of those who provided input to the manuscript. Adam Berger, Craig Berger, Nancy Berger, Cheryl McGuire, and Carol and Marc Rubinger listened, reviewed, critiqued, and encouraged.

Lance would like to recognize Steven Werner, who introduced him to the Yankees and to baseball. Steven is the ultimate Yankee fan with an endless capacity to discuss and dissect the past, present, and future of the team. Lance also recognizes Gene Werner, who joined him, while growing up in Brooklyn, in watching many baseball games.

Dorothy would like to thank Max Turk, her father, for introducing her to the Yankees as a young girl. She spent many Sunday afternoon doubleheaders sitting on the hard, backless benches in the bleachers in Yankee Stadium taunting the pitchers in the bull pen and hoping that Mickey Mantle would recognize his most avid admirer.

We would like to extend special appreciation to Ruth and Henry Berger, Florence Turk, Steven McGuire, Alejandra Gimenez Berger, and Alexandra Berger for tolerating our baseball mania.

Introduction:
How Does an Organization
Dominate Its Industry
for 80 Years?

If you're a Yankee fan, or if you're not a Yankee fan—you have to admit, we're winners.

—Paul O'Neill, Yankee outfielder from 1993
to 2002, after the 2000 World Series

I've been a management consultant for 25 years and I know how rare it is for a company to dominate an industry for more than a few years. Customers and technologies change, and new competitors rise up to challenge the great companies that have grown complacent because they thought that the lush days of success would last forever. This makes the Yankee record over the past eight decades all the more amazing. Since 1921, the Yankees have been in the World Series 39 times and have won the championship 26 times. No other team comes close—the nearest team has won only nine championships. It may not be exaggerating to say that no other team in any sport in history has a comparable long-term record of winning championships. Certainly, being a dominant force for eight decades is a feat achieved by few corporations in American history.

Whether you love or hate the Yankees, it is clear to anyone who looks at the history of the team from an objective, business perspective that they are not just another sports team. Something about the Yankee organization enables them to win decade after decade, despite changing players, changing owners, and changing managers. This book argues that the secret is a set of 14 principles that represent the Yankees' best management practices. The principles emerged in the 1920s under the leadership of owner Jacob Ruppert, and have been developed and refined by later owners and management teams ever since. The Yankees described in this book represent an amalgam of successful teams from their long history.

The 14 management principles that emerged from my study of the history of the team's success are applicable to any organization. That is why you don't have to be a Yankee fan or even know anything about baseball to benefit from the management wisdom of this sports dynasty. All that is required is an interest in building a competitive advantage in your company. The iconic characters—from owners to managers to players—who served in the various Yankee organizations are symbolic of the types of people we manage and work with every day in our work environments. The Yankees, in the context of this book, are a metaphor for sustained organizational and business excellence.

The Big Yankee Management Myth: Buying Championships?

Not everyone will agree that the 14 principles (listed later in this Introduction) are the basis of the Yankees' eight-decade track record. One common (and misleading) myth is that since the Yankee owners have always had deep pockets they could simply buy any superstars they wanted from their competitors (as they famously bought Babe Ruth from the Boston Red Sox). Big contracts in baseball garner many headlines and much ink in newspapers across the nation, and often, unfortunately, that is what most people read and hear about the Yankees. But this is a very simplistic way of looking at Yankee success, and it dismisses many other core values and guiding principles of the dynasty. If you don't look beyond the myth that the Yankees simply buy all the best players, you will deprive yourself of powerful management knowledge that could help your organization build its own dynasty.

While it's true that under George Steinbrenner the Yankees have had the biggest payroll in baseball, offering big salaries to lure superstars from other teams is only one component of their overall strategy and culture. The reality is that with the exception of Babe Ruth and a few others, "buying" superstars has played a small overall role in Yankee history. In fact, although they acquired stars from other teams, they purchased no existing superstars from any other major league team after the acquisition of Babe Ruth and Waite Hoyt from the Boston Red Sox in the early 1920s until they outbid their competitors for the great pitcher Catfish Hunter in 1974. This was due to many factors. First, the reserve clause, a league regulation that bound players to their current teams, did not permit any team to buy the services of a player directly from the player. Second, no other team traded them a superstar or sold them one. Third, the Yankees focused their scouting and player development energies on their extensive farm system, and had no reason to look outside the organization for talent.

In 1974, the era of free agency blossomed. Originally, owner George Steinbrenner was against free agency because of its potential negative financial impact on the team. However, he soon realized that the depletion of his farm system under the watch of the previous owner, the Columbia Broadcasting System (CBS), left him with no choice but to pursue this route to resuscitate the dynasty. He simply had no internal resources to build a winner. Steinbrenner ultimately recognized that free agency could be used to the Yankees' advantage. Since then, starting with Catfish Hunter, the Yankees have taken advantage of the free agent market to buy talent.

However, even if the Yankees wanted to buy enough superstars to fill the team, some superstars have no interest in becoming a Yankee, many do not meet Yankee standards off the field, and many other teams have sufficient resources to retain their own superstars. The same is true in any business. Another reality is that the supply of superstars available at any moment in time is relatively small, and the available superstar pool does not have players for every position on the field. So even with deep pockets in the recent decades of free agency, it has been impossible for the Yankees to buy a complete team of superstars. But they haven't needed to because, like every great business, they have an ability to develop great talent from within the organization.

Where Does the Yankees' Star Talent Come From?

Most of the Yankee greats, over the eight-decade history of the dynasty, were homegrown and developed *within* the organization. The reason the Yankees' payroll is so large is that high salaries are required to keep great players *after* the Yankees discover them and turn them into superstars. Mickey Mantle was plucked up by astute scouting right after high school graduation. Lou Gehrig was signed while playing for Columbia University. More recently, Derek Jeter and Bernie Williams came up through the farm system, as did superstar player Mariano Rivera and star Jorge Posada. (Later in the book I'll explain the difference between a "star" and a "superstar" and why your company needs at least one of each.) The Yankees' recent 10 straight years of postseason play have been powered by homegrown talent.

In the early years of the dynasty, after the purchase of Babe Ruth's contract in 1920, the Yankees used their superior ability to assess talent and to trade and to buy stars and solid players from other major league teams, minor league teams, and a variety of other sources. While homing in on high-quality talent, they removed players who were not solid contributors. Once they adopted and mastered the development of their own farm system in the 1940s, all of their superstars and most of their stars and solid players were homegrown. Potential superstar and star talent was discovered in high schools, colleges, and bush leagues by astute Yankee scouts. They were able to strengthen their roster through shrewd trades for players from their competitors' parent or farm system teams. Additionally, the Yankees' superior assessment capabilities enabled them to capture fading superstars and stars and to deploy them in highly specialized roles.

Dynasties are built on much more than a few superstars. Money can keep superstars on a team but it can't buy the genuine teamwork and winning culture that creates a cohesive, winning organization decade after decade. Money spent unwisely can lead to high-priced failure. For example, the rosters of highly paid players failed to reach postseason play between 1965 and 1975 and then again between 1982 and 1994. During these periods, teams with smaller payrolls were more competitive and the Yankees were ridiculed for their poor performance. No one could say then that the Yankees were buying championships. I believe that when the Yankees failed to win it was because they did not follow their own principles. Likewise, Yankee success has been the result of following the key principles that emerged at the beginning of the dynasty and has developed until the present day.

The Lesson for Business Managers: You Don't Need a Yankee-Size Payroll to Build a Superstar Team

The Yankees' success has created a halo effect around their players and the perception among the players, media, and fans that the team is comprised of all superstars. The reality is the Yankees are a superstar team rather than a team of all superstars. For most of their history, the Yankees have been a blend of a few superstars, several stars, and many solid players. The Yankees' mystique was created by Yankee teams that played the "Yankee Way."

It is true that organizations need some minimal level of payroll to have any chance of competing on an ongoing basis with Yankee-like opponents; it is not necessary, however, to have the highest payroll. With a reasonably competitive payroll, your organization can be a top contender in its industry by more efficiently applying basic Yankee success principles to your own business situation. The secret to the Yankees' success is not mythical. It is the result of a set of 14 sound business principles for managing talent that were applied over an 80-year period. A shrewd manager can use the Yankee principles to create a winning tradition in his own organization and do it much more cheaply and more effectively than his Yankee-like competitors.

How I Came to Write This Book

I am a loyal Yankee fan. I have followed the team for 50 years of the eight-decade dynasty. I have tracked the team longer than the current owner, George Steinbrenner. I have suffered "the slings and arrows of outrageous fortune" during losing years and celebrated and rejoiced with the team in the successful ones. During this time, I have often wondered about, discussed, and debated the secret of the Yankee magic. How could one team enjoy so much success, and be so much more successful than any of their competition? The opportunity to unlock these secrets first presented itself 24 years ago when I started my first management consulting assignment with Major League Baseball (MLB). It was at the beginning of my career with a large management consulting firm, and I was assigned to assist in the design of a compensation structure for the Commissioner's Office, American League, National League, Player Relations Committee (labor relations), and marketing arm (then called Major League Baseball Promotion Corporation). I could not believe my good fortune. Although I simultaneously enjoyed working with great companies like General Electric, GTE, International Paper, PepsiCo, and Perdue Farms, my heart was with Major League Baseball.

In order to complete my assignment, I was given direct access to key executives at MLB and any documents relative to accomplishing my goal. The first part of the project entailed writing the job descriptions of Baseball Commissioner Bowie Kuhn and the presidents of the National and American Leagues. To capture the essence of these jobs, it was necessary for me to probe into the core of the game itself. I reviewed current and historical information on all the teams as well as the executive structure of baseball. An avid fan thus became an insider. My consultant's expertise afforded me the opportunity to explore, and understand, the nature of baseball from a strategic, organizational, and people perspective. On a more personal level, I was able to look for the source of the Yankee dynasty within the core of Major League Baseball, a most reliable source. Strikingly, I found that the current Yankee organization has a great deal in common with the other owners of the team since the 1920s. The core management principles that were formulated at the beginning of the dynasty were retained, embellished, and expanded by subsequent generations of owners. These later owners studied the successful lessons of the past and were willing to reapply them.

Perhaps my most productive source of information on the Yankees was Bob Fishel. Fishel had been an integral part of the Yankee organization for many years, and had witnessed all of the Yankee ownership periods. At the end of one of my sessions with Fishel, he suggested, to my surprise, that I write a book that combined my fan's perspective with my experiences in consulting to blue-chip businesses and MLB. The book would be a unique perspective on why the Yankees were so dominant over such a long time period. Fishel felt that the Yankees' history of success could provide managers in any business with a set of organization and management guidelines that they could replicate. He told me that blips in the Yankee dynasty occurred when the team lost sight of their established success principles.

Although I completed my first project and continued to work with Major League Baseball, I "dropped the ball" and never attempted to write the book. However, I never forgot Fishel's challenge. Twenty-four years later, after completing my fifth management book, I recalled Fishel's challenge and casually mentioned it to my senior editor, Richard Narramore, and editor, Andrew Littell. They encouraged me to pursue the project.

The Three Key Yankee Ownership Regimes and Two "Dark Ages"

In 1915, Jacob Ruppert and Tillinghast L'Hommedieu Huston bought the Yankees from Frank Ferrell and Bill Devery. Ferrell and Devery had brought the defunct Baltimore Orioles to New York in 1903 and had losing seasons, not to mention a dearth of loyal fans, while playing at the Polo Grounds, the New York Giants' home field. Jacob Ruppert, who was used to running successful businesses, was determined to change the franchise's fortunes and at the same time increase his own financial empire. Ruppert was an entrepreneurial and dynamic owner with a philosophy and passion for winning. He hired the demanding and innovative Miller Huggins as manager in 1918, bought out Huston's shares in 1923, and constructed the final piece of the foundation when he began to articulate a set of informal operating principles based on organizations that had been successful in the past. "Acquire the superstar," one of the earliest operating principles, led to the purchase of Babe Ruth from the Boston Red Sox in 1920. Only one year later, with the acquisition of four key Boston star pitchers, the Yankees played in their first World Series and the dynasty was established. Ruppert's foundation was reconstructed in each of two later reigns in the dynasty. The second reign was Del Webb/Dan Topping and the third is George Steinbrenner.

Of course, even great corporations have lean years, and the Yankees are no exception. The Yankee dynasty includes two "dark ages" (periods when the team did not compete in postseason play). The first occurred between 1965 and 1975 when CBS owned the team. The second occurred between 1982 and 1994 during the reign of the current principal owner, George Steinbrenner. As I mentioned earlier, I believe these fallow years were a direct result of the Yankees not adhering to their traditional principles for success outlined in this book. During the CBS era, the foundation was broken largely because of owner disinterest, lack of player leadership, and a failure to effectively apply key principles of talent management. During the second blip, the foundation was weakened by Steinbrenner's lack of focus on staffing key positions (pitchers and catchers) with at least star-quality players and his employment of a field manager (Billy Martin) who did not reflect the traditional Yankee professional characteristics and citizenship values.

Executive Summary of the Fourteen Yankee Success Principles

The 14 principles described in this book are grouped around three main themes: leadership, processes, and culture. Together they constitute a road map for building your own dynasty.

Part I—Leadership Establishes the Foundation

PRINCIPLE 1: CULTIVATE OWNERSHIP VALUES FROM THE TOP DOWN

Winning owners have characteristics and behaviors that set them apart from their peers. Most Yankee owners brought an opportunistic spirit to the team and added their special touch to the Yankee tradition. Starting with Jacob Ruppert, we examine the entrepreneurial behaviors that translate into creating a winning culture. These owners were successful in influencing team results through the selection of a management staff built on ownership principles and by shaping player behaviors on and off the field. They managed to instill in all their employees the desire to win. All employees become an integral part of achieving organizational success; they are "empowered owners." All employees of the Yankee organization are expected to embrace the principal owner's values and competencies, which are passed down through the executive office and field (first-level) manager.

PRINCIPLE 2: HIRE THE BEST FRONTLINE MANAGERS YOU CAN FIND
(THEY'RE THE MOST IMPORTANT PEOPLE IN YOUR ORGANIZATION)

The field manager, or first-level manager, represents the key formal figure (frontline authority) of an organization's structure. This person is the face of the organization that each member of the team sees every day. The team's performance is heavily determined by the operational and strategic decisions made by the field manager. The field manager is the bridge from ownership and management to the players.

The first-level manager in your organization is responsible for supervising the employees who develop or sell services or products. With the authority of the owners, the first-level manager plans, organizes, and/or integrates a function or set of employee activities. The first-level manager must possess all the professional, citizenship, and leadership competencies exemplified by ownership to help your organization create and sustain excellence.

PRINCIPLE 3: FORMALLY RECOGNIZE YOUR INFORMAL LEADERS

Every company or team should have formally recognized team leaders. They are the individuals who excel at their jobs, who inspire others to excel, and who display behaviors that bring credit to the team. They are first recognized and respected as leaders by their teammates. Organizations must acknowledge and support these informal leaders. In baseball, this person is designated captain. The captain is a role model who links traditional winning ways to current conditions. This chapter looks at the Yankee captains' important characteristics, examines the role these men played on their team, and looks at the role of the captain in a modern business setting.

Part II—Processes for Developing and Maintaining a Dynasty

PRINCIPLE 4: SET THE BAR HIGHER THAN YOUR PEOPLE HAVE EVER SEEN IT: QUANTITATIVE PERFORMANCE MEASURES

Every organization must have clear and established winning standards for the organization as a whole, and for each employee. Everyone must be clear as to what constitutes winning. For the Yankees, winning is equated with a World Championship. To repeatedly achieve this lofty goal, all Yankee players must accept that specific measures of individual accomplishment are subordinate to winning the World Series. Expectations for player performance will be high, concrete, and linked to the team goal. For the organization and the players the measures must be unequivocal.

Yankee team success is also measured by the size of the fan base relative to other baseball and sports teams. The owner's goal is to sell out the ballpark and to dominate the airwaves. Success is also equated with the variety and numbers of Yankee products sold in a multitude of outlets. The size of the fan base is the foundation for financial competitive advantage, which in turn translates into increased ability to reinvest in the team by securing and paying for the best available talent, which ultimately results in additional fans. The Yankee goal is to put the most competitive team on the field not only to win championships but to attract and retain the greatest number of fans. In the corporate world, the fan base is akin to the customer pool.

Often, an organization will compare itself to another organization, identifying that organization as its main competition. For any organization this means knowing the strengths, weaknesses, and success potential of the closest competitor and using these parameters to stimulate a spirited rivalry. This chapter looks at the high bar the Yankees have set for themselves throughout the dynasty, the definition of success at the organizational and individual levels, and the effect that having a competitive foil has had on Yankee success.

PRINCIPLE 5: MAKE ORGANIZATIONAL COMPETENCIES THE HEART OF YOUR APPRAISAL PROCESS: QUALITATIVE PERFORMANCE MEASURES

For the Yankees as well as your organization, competencies are the foundation for winning. Competencies are the observable and measurable skills, values, and behaviors that contribute to enhanced employee performance and organizational success. Competencies must be clearly defined, articulated, and embedded throughout your organization.

Earlier chapters discuss how Yankee competencies, as established and exemplified by the principal owner, are key components in the selection of the field manager and team captains. This fifth principle explores how the Yankees use their competencies in the appraisal, selection, and development processes for every member of the organization. These competencies include professional, leadership, and citizenship skills.

PRINCIPLE 6: MAKE EVERYONE ON THE TEAM A TALENT SCOUT

One of the major sources of differentiation possessed by the Yankees is their ability to scout and assess talent. This chapter focuses on how the Yankees are able to consistently maintain a high-quality team through their own special approach. We look at their scouting methods and the importance of employing talented talent scouts. We also examine a Yankee secret strategy: Everyone on the team is a talent scout.

Your organization can expand its scouting field beyond the formal conduits by instilling talent assessment and scouting as an organizational value. Employees must understand their potential critical role in bringing fresh talent into your company.

PRINCIPLE 7: CREATE A BALANCE OF SUPERSTARS, STARS, AND SOLID PERFORMERS:
ASSESSING AND CLASSIFYING YOUR EMPLOYEES

You hear it all the time: "The Yankees are a team of all-stars." "The Yankees just buy other teams' superstars." "They have a superstar at every position." However, despite what many detractors believe to be the key to the Yankee dynasty, there are not enough superstars in the baseball player pool for the Yankees to buy and field a team of only superstars. The Yankee dynasty teams have been developed around a blend of players at varying performance levels: superstars, stars, and solid performers. Granted, the Yankees know the value of having a few superstars on the team, but far more important to Yankee success is how they use various types of players to win baseball games. This chapter looks at how the Yankees continually classify and reclassify players and use these classifications to create a dynastic team with the right blend of talent. Every organization, including the Yankees (despite its reputation to the contrary), has finite dollars to be spent on its workforce, so it must use its money wisely.

Principle 8: Establish Your Talent Strategy and Fill in the Gaps

This chapter describes how the Yankees use talent classifications (superstars, stars, solid players, oddballs) to build a comprehensive inventory of players inside and outside the organization. The inventory enables the Yankees to implement a unique three-part strategy:

1. Identify and retain superstars in their organization and/or acquire them from competitor organizations.
2. Ensure the battery (key positions—pitcher and catcher) has at least star and potential star backups.
3. Make certain that everyone on the team is rated as at least a solid player.

This strategy first took shape in the Jacob Ruppert era. This chapter discusses how it has evolved and how the Yankees implement each step of the strategy to guarantee that they field the most competitive team possible.

Principle 9: Create a Solid Farm System: Train and Develop Your People

Since 1929, one of the primary reasons for the continuation of the Yankee dynasty has been the farm system. In the farm system, minor league teams feed talent through the organization up to the parent club, the major league team. During this process, young talented players are developed, their skills are honed, and they learn the values of the Yankee organization. A strong farm system can cost-effectively build its superstar and star base and even trade surplus talent to fill its voids. Continual talent development protects an organization against competitor raids and makes it less susceptible to being held hostage to excessive salary demands. This chapter looks at how the Yankee organization has continually brought new players into the farm system to maintain a steady stream of talent to the major league club.

Principle 10: Pay Your People Based on Their Contribution to Organization Success

Babe Ruth said, "Someday every player will be paid his true worth." Ruth's words finally rang true with the death of the reserve clause. Today a player's salary should be based on his current and projected talent classification as a gauge of his actual and potential contribution to the team. The Yankees use this assessment of contribution as the basis for making decisions on the salaries of players on their major and minor league teams and prospective players from a myriad of other sources. In order for this approach to be effective, the team must have accurate player assessments and a detailed knowledge of specific talent requirements. The latter typically comes from an organization-wide bench strength summary and talent management plan. Twice in their history, for extended periods of time, the Yankees failed to follow this disciplined approach. The result was a large payroll and mediocre team performance.

Most organizations cannot afford to spend payroll dollars haphazardly. Missteps can lead to inability to attract star talent or, even worse, loss of your top people to competitor organizations. For this reason, your organization must remember that the first principle in compensation management is not spending more than you can afford. The second principle is spending what you can afford wisely. Whatever your budget, wisely spending your money is the key to sustainable competitive success.

Principle 11: Make the Superstar the Focal Point of Your Organization

A superstar is a commodity in short supply. This makes the superstar a very special ingredient in a talent management program. That is why we single this person out for special attention. Superstars generally comprise only around 2 percent to 4 percent of the number of players in any given year. Their value to their team is immeasurable. Even without looking at statistics, the superstar's presence alone inspires confidence. When he is absent from the starting lineup due to injury, heads begin to droop in the dugout and mistakes are made on the field. The level of play of the remaining team members is considerably lower when the superstar isn't playing his position. Now imagine if that superstar is out of the lineup for good, lured away by a competitor. Not only is the competition much stronger in that position, but also the original team is leaderless. Talk about competitive advantage.

Hiring your competitor's superstars weakens the direct competitor's strength, demoralizes all competitors, greatly improves your team, and creates media focus that heightens fan (customer) interest. And the Yankees are the best in the baseball world at doing exactly that. Paradoxically, however, the Yankees did not pirate a superstar from a competitor between the early 1920s (Babe Ruth and Waite Hoyt) and 1975 (Catfish Hunter). Since then they have used superstar acquisition in a highly selective mode. When the Yankee farm system started to produce high-quality talent, the Yankees added superstar retention to their strategy of superstar acquisition.

Part III—Design Your Culture for Success

PRINCIPLE 12: DIVERSIFY YOUR TALENT POOL

Diversity is a success principle that evolved under George Steinbrenner. Until the Steinbrenner era, the Yankees lagged in expanding the ethnicity of the team. Baseball talent was what intrigued Steinbrenner, not the color of his players' skin. He knew that to fully implement the Yankee talent strategy no group of people could be excluded from the pool of available talent. Eight years after Jackie Robinson broke the color barrier, Elston Howard became the first African-American Yankee player in 1955. The Yankee dynasty was diminished by its failure to consider quality talent from all sources when their competitors were doing so. The failure of the Yankees to expand their pool of diverse players in the 1940s and 1950s reduced the number of superstars and stars available to the team in the late 1960s and early 1970s. This shortsightedness contributed to the Yankees' first dark age from 1965 through 1975. Today the Yankees are a blend of African-American, Latino, Asian, and Caucasian players. This diversity has been translated into on-field and box-office success. There are no restrictions on where they will search for talent. They know that they must search even in the most unconventional places to bolster talent at all levels of the organization.

PRINCIPLE 13: CELEBRATE YOUR HISTORY, HEROES, AND LEGENDS: CREATING TRADITIONS OF EXCELLENCE

Perhaps no other organization is so filled with myth and legend as the Yankees. The names of the players, their monuments in center field at Yankee Stadium, the retired numbers, the stories, the pinstripe uniform, the World Championship banners, the rings they wear, all of it is part of what people think about when they think about the Yankees. This is not by accident. The Yankee organization has gone to great lengths to promote their history and tradition of excellence. The Yankees tell their stories, publicly celebrate past heroes and legends, and use their past successes to persuade current and prospective players to believe that they are destined to win. The Yankees are more than a team. They are an American success story that has captured the imaginations of people worldwide. On and off the field, the Yankees have been successful at selling themselves. Beginning with the Ruppert era, each primary owner embraced promotional rules.

PRINCIPLE 14: BOLDLY PROMOTE YOUR TRADITION OF EXCELLENCE

The baseball universe expects the New York Yankees to be World Champions every year. Each season brings an expectation that this dynasty will endure. The Yankees have done an incredible job of promoting this winning tradition to all members of the organization, from batboy to players to management to fans and the media. The Yankees began with two organizational promotional goals: associating the Yankee brand with winning, and becoming an employer of choice. They accomplish these goals using a four-step strategy: focus on team accomplishments; focus on the superstar; pick colorful and committed hucksters to spread your message; and package the team image in a classical and epic-evoking environment. The Yankee brand was built using these four strategies, and the organization has become one of the most recognizable in the world. People associate the Yankees with winning.

The 14 principles are as applicable to the world of business and to your company as they are to the Yankees. May this book help you build a dynasty!

PART I

Leadership Establishes the Foundation

CHAPTER

1

Cultivate Ownership Values from the Top Down

Winning owners have characteristics and behaviors that set them apart from their peers. Most Yankee owners brought an opportunistic spirit to the team and added their special touch to enriching the Yankee tradition. Starting with Jacob Ruppert, we examine the entrepreneurial behaviors that translate into creating a winning culture. These owners were successful in influencing team results through the selection of a management staff built on ownership principles and by shaping player behaviors on and off the field. They managed to instill in all employees the desire to win. All employees become an integral part of achieving organizational success; they are "empowered owners." All employees of the Yankee organization are expected to embrace the principal owner's values and competencies, which are passed down through the executive office and field (first-level) manager.

Top of the Heap

The success of the Yankees, like the success of any business organization, begins with its ownership structure. The Yankee system of ownership functions on two levels: the legal owners, represented by the principal owner, and the empowered owners, employees who demonstrate ownership of their responsibilities and embrace the values of the organization.

The first level consists of the people who have the recognized authority, and invested capital, to determine the direction of the institution. They are the legal owners. The principal owner represents all the legal owners and is the publicly visible and authoritative force that drives the team. The most influential principal Yankee owners have been, in chronological order, Jacob Ruppert, Del Webb and Dan Topping, and George Steinbrenner.

Interestingly, all the Yankee principal owners had chairman-level involvement with other high-profile businesses—they were not merely owners of baseball teams. Ruppert had Knickerbocker Beer; Del Webb ran a construction company that built office buildings, factories, hotels, and veterans' hospitals; Dan Topping ran Anaconda Steel; and George Steinbrenner has served as chairman of the board of the American Ship Building Company. They were equally at home in a traditional corporate boardroom and in the Yankee front office.

In the corporate world, the chairman of the board and/or CEO plays the owner's role. The list of corporate counterparts to George Steinbrenner would include entrepreneurial top executives like Mary Kay Ash (Mary Kay Inc. cosmetics), Bill Gates (Microsoft Corporation), Frank Perdue (Perdue Farms chicken), and Michael Dell (Dell Inc. computers).

However, the success of the principal owner of the Yankees lies not only in his own skills but in his ability to instill in his employees the desire to win; all employees must take ownership of organizational success just as the invested owners do. As empowered owners, the employees make up the Yankees' second level of ownership. They must adopt most of the success characteristics of the principal owners for the team to win. In this chapter, we look at the ownership characteristics of the principal owner, the tremendous importance of the owner's selection of first-level and field-level managers, and the empowered ownership of the employees of the Yankee organization.

Yankee history must be framed in terms of its ownership structure since 1915 when the foundation for the dynasty was laid by Jacob Ruppert. Ruppert was an entrepreneurial, dynamic owner who embodied all the behaviors that will be discussed later. Ruppert built the Yankee winning tradition as the team won 10 pennants and seven World Championships under his stewardship. His reign has had an enduring effect in shaping the behaviors of future principal owners and in triggering the concept of player ownership as a factor in team success.

Yankee Ownership Since 1915

There have been four sets of owners since 1915. Three of these built the dynasty. Each of the successful ownership sets was represented by a strong leader, and these leaders were linked by shared characteristics. These leaders are the principal owners. Jacob Ruppert's management and leadership DNA is the template for the ensuing Yankee principal owners. The concept of the principal owner is central to the Yankees building a dynasty.

The four ownership eras are:

1. 1915–1945: Colonel Jacob Ruppert and Colonel Tillinghast L'Hommedieu Huston (1915–1922); Jacob Ruppert (1923–1938); Ruppert estate (1939–1944).

2. 1945–1964: Dan Topping, Del Webb, and Larry MacPhail (1945–1947).

3. 1965–1972: Columbia Broadcasting System (CBS).

4. 1973–present: George Steinbrenner (head of limited partnership).

See box for an overview of the four Yankee ownership eras since 1915.

YANKEE OWNERS SINCE 1915

OWNER	WON/ LOST RECORD	PERCENTAGE	CHAMPIONSHIPS
RUPPERT/HUSTON	553–475	.538	0
RUPPERT	1,604–1,103	.593	7
RUPPERT ESTATE	579–342	.629	3
TOPPING/WEBB/MACPHAIL	1,916–1,329	.590	10
CBS	636–649	.495	0
STEINBRENNER	2,525–2,039	.553	6

The Linkage Is Broken

The linkage of principal owners in the mold of Jacob Ruppert was broken when CBS purchased the team. The Yankee dynasty faltered under CBS ownership. Under the CBS ownership, the Yankees did not have a principal owner. As part of a broad policy of business diversification, CBS purchased the Yankees along with other enterprises such as publishing, educational toys, and piano manufacturing. As a small piece in a huge empire, the Yankees existed to serve the larger interests of CBS. Corporate ownership proved the wrong way to run a winning baseball team. The Yankees were an insignificant part of a much greater enterprise that had more important issues than just winning baseball games. The team lost its winning focus.

Rebuilding a Dynasty

What makes the Yankees such an outstanding organization is their success through most of the three principal ownership eras. There was an initial rebuilding of the dynasty after Steinbrenner purchased the team, and the team regained its winning form after three seasons under his stewardship. The Yankees underwent another dark spell under Steinbrenner from 1982 to 1994 when the team was destabilized by Steinbrenner's inability to maintain a stable management structure. The general manager and field manager positions were revolving doors with no manager fully claiming Steinbrenner's support. Additionally, the team failed to staff some key positions (pitcher and catcher) with high-quality talent.

After a turbulent era during which he temporarily relinquished control of the team, Steinbrenner began to surround himself with people who more closely reflected the Yankee Way. During Steinbrenner's period of suspension he was forced to put greater operational control of the team in the hands of his management, and the on-field results were very positive. Ultimately he placed Brian Cashman in the general manager position and Joe Torre in the field manager's role. Cashman, with the support of other high-quality executives like Gene Michael, provided Torre with the players he needed, and Steinbrenner allowed them to perform their roles, confident they had the traditional Yankee values and competencies to restore the dynasty. The Yankees again became a team in the truest sense with Steinbrenner, management, and players fulfilling their roles in the Yankee Way. The Yankee dynasty was reenergized, and 10 straight postseason appearances and four World Championships were the result.

The first step to understanding why the Yankees have enjoyed such sustained accomplishments is to examine the characteristics that all successful principal owners have exhibited. Since we are talking about the Yankees, it should come as no surprise that the most important characteristic is the desire to win.

The Principal Owner

Like most successful CEOs, all Yankee owners share a passion for winning. Yankee principal owners were all successful businessmen before purchasing the team and recognized how winning businesses functioned. They bought the team with the expectation of establishing a winner. Losing was not acceptable. But for the Yankees, success was defined not simply by having a winning record, but by being the best, possessing the number one spot: World Champions. This passion has permeated all Yankee teams and has been most visibly reflected in their expectation to win every time. It is this *expectation* and respect for the highest level of accomplishment for the team that is the first competency upon which the other Yankee success characteristics are built. The Yankees don't play for second place, and this measure of success begins with the principal owner and permeates the entire organization. Even the batboys know that without a trip to the World Series, it's a losing season.

The Owners' Competencies

My research on the Yankees and my conversations with Bob Fishel about all the Yankee owners revealed that, in addition to this passion for winning, the owners also shared some remarkably similar values, behaviors, and traits. These shared characteristics, or principal ownership competencies, have shaped Yankee success. These additional competencies fall into the categories of professional skills, citizenship in the organization, and leadership. Let's look at each of these categories.

Professional Skills

- *Financial knowledge.* Strategic insight into what the team must do to optimize its profitability.

- *Knowledge of the game.* Understanding of on- and off-field baseball rules and how these rules can be successfully used for business advantage.

- *Organizational skill.* Capabilities to build an organization with a trusted staff, to delegate authority, to support management, and to enforce the rules and traditions of the team.

- *Marketing the Yankee image.* Ability to convey a clear and positive perception of the team to the public, league, team, other owners, and all other employees.

- *Talent management.* Ability to select and groom talent, including general managers, field managers, and players. The owner must know the competencies necessary for excellence and use them to accurately assess, cultivate, and deploy managers, staff, and players based on these requirements.

Citizenship

- *Love of the organization.* Willingness to put the team's success first in all financial, staffing, and marketing considerations.

- *Respect for tradition and readiness to learn from the past.* The owner's recognition that he has purchased more than just another team. He has become an elite member of an elite club who is entrusted to learn from and maintain a tradition of excellence.

- *Commitment to decorum*. Willingness to enforce on- and off-field behaviors that reflect good taste and a positive baseball image. The owner establishes standards for on- and off-field dress, including physical appearance as well as how fans, media, and players are treated. While the Yankees accommodate some cultural differences in the players' demeanors, their orientation is always toward the traditional, neat, pinstripe look on-field and conservative dress when not at the ballpark. Yankee personnel understand that they are representatives, and images, of a winning tradition.

Leadership

- *Team orientation*. Unites all staff to play as a single team.
- *Sense of urgency*. Energetically pursues goals and instills urgency throughout the team through communication and action.
- *Opportunism and risk taking*. Anticipates, perseveres, and takes decisive action under conditions of uncertainty (risk) to enhance the team's competitive advantage.
- *Innovation*. Generates and implements personally or through others novel ideas that will create value for the team.
- *Visibility*. Takes a high-profile position at critical times within and outside the organization to explain team activities, support actions and decisions, and represent the winning tradition of the Yankees.
- *Optimism*. Believes and encourages others to believe that the team will always prevail.

The passion for achievement, combined with professional skills, citizenship in the organization, and leadership skills as portrayed by the principal owner are the basis for the selection of all other Yankee employees, including general manager (chief operating officer), the field manager (first-level manager), coaches (trainers and developers), scouts (recruiters), and players (all employees).

Selection of Senior Executives

The roles of senior operating executives (typically called president or general manager) have varied under the different principal owners, but they've had one thing in common: Each principal owner has had other businesses that have consumed a great deal of his time, and while the owners have retained visible control of the Yankee organization, they also needed a full-time operative to translate their philosophy of winning on a daily basis. They needed trusted individuals, and they selected people they could count on for their business as well as baseball skills. These people had to embrace, reflect, and advocate for the principal ownership competencies. In most cases, the general managers either bought or were given a stake in the team so they could be actual team owners.

Colonel Jacob Ruppert, the first owner in the Yankee dynasty, selected a trusted friend and experienced baseball man for his business manager, who later became the Yankees' president. Edward G. Barrow came to the Yankee front office with varied business experiences in newspaper work, theatrical production, and hotel proprietorship, in addition to an equally diverse baseball experience as baseball park concessionaire, minor league manager, minor league president, and major league manager. Ruppert had total faith that Barrow represented his values, and entrusted him with the complete operation of the front office. Even after Ruppert's death when the ownership sat in Ruppert's estate, the dynasty prospered under Barrow's stewardship.

For the 25 years that Barrow held the general manager's position, all operative decisions emanated from him.

Webb and Topping, the second ownership era, chose George Weiss as their general manager. Weiss, more than any other person, was responsible for the unprecedented success of the Yankees from the mid-1930s until the mid-1960s. In 1932, after gaining experience as general manager with the Baltimore team of the International League, Weiss became farm director of the Yankees. In that position, he kept a stream of talent flowing to the major league team for the next 15 years. In 1948, Weiss became general manager of the Yankees with the understanding from Webb and Topping that he would continue to infuse the team with top talent. Webb and Topping ran their other businesses and entrusted Weiss to run the Yankees. Weiss instilled the Webb/Topping passion for winning throughout the team.

George Steinbrenner chose Gabe Paul as his first president and right-hand man. Paul had 50 years of baseball experience, and Steinbrenner knew that Paul had the network, respect, and intuition to obtain the necessary talent to turn what was then a losing franchise into a winner. Paul also demanded a financial interest in the team. He had the self-confidence and strong convictions needed to run the team, even with Steinbrenner's periodic intrusion. He ultimately built a championship team. In 1978, Paul quit the team after tiring of the upheaval caused by the interactions of George Steinbrenner, Billy Martin (field manager), and Reggie Jackson (superstar player). Steinbrenner hired and fired many presidents and general managers until he named Brian Cashman to the position in 1998. Cashman was one of the Yankees' own, having worked for the Yankees since interning as a college student in the front office in 1986, and had spent five years as assistant general manager under two general managers. The 31-year-old Cashman was groomed in the Yankee Way.

All these senior executives shared their principal owners' passion for winning and accepted and demonstrated the traits and characteristics that had made the owners themselves successful businessmen. Selection of a proven and loyal trouper with ownership-shared values to run the organization is a primary criterion for success.

Selection of the Field Manager

The principal owner is also accountable for directly selecting and/or approving the hiring of the field manager. The field manager, like the first-level manager in any organization, is the primary interface between employees and management. An employee's knowledge of his organization, expectations for success, and adherence to cultural expectations are shaped by daily interactions with this first level of authority. On a baseball team, the principal owner can ensure that managers are selected based on their own requirements by directly participating in the hiring process. In a more traditional organization the expectations of the principal owner must be put in writing and used by others to make the appropriate selection decisions.

In the eight decades of the dynasty, the Yankee field managers have had relatively little success in managing other teams. None of the six dominant field managers who operated during the dynasty had ever previously won a World Series. One manager had won a league pennant, and two had won divisional titles on teams other than the Yankees, but none had ever demonstrated with another team the kind of success demanded by the Yankees. Collectively with the Yankees they won 24 World Championships and 34 league pennants.

One might argue that charismatic and well-funded owners could contribute disproportionately to the success of the team, but this argument begs the question of how so many managers with poor performance could be selected in the first place. The answer lies in the fact that, like general managers, field managers had to embrace the values of the principal owner. Possession of these values was more important in a field manager than winning experience with a previous team because they related more to winning with the Yankees. This meant that the principal owners had to have a clear vision of specific success characteristics of the field managers. Ultimately they selected managers who fit their profile for winning with the Yankees rather than those who necessarily had a prior record of winning. The managers had to have the professional skills for managing a team as well as the citizenship and leadership skills that differentiated the Yankees from their competitors. The principal owners, with the support of their general managers, were willing to take a risk. Risk taking, of course, is a competency of principal owners.

The fundamental concept for establishing a dynasty is that the template, or DNA, for winning is manufactured at the top of the organization. The DNA is then used in determining the selection of the management. Additionally, while hierarchical organizations have many levels, the principal owner must have a direct connection to the selection of first-level line managers, since they are the most significant operating component of the organization.

The Empowered Owners

But it isn't just the first-level or field managers who must carry this DNA. All employees of the Yankee organization are expected to embrace the principal owner's values and competencies, which have been passed down through the executive office and field (first-level) manager. Players can demonstrate ownership by:

- Focusing all individual efforts on helping the team win the World Championship.

- Cultivating professional skills.

- Embracing the Yankee citizenship requirements previously listed.

- Constructively influencing and supporting management and other players.

By instilling his core beliefs in all team members, the principal owner empowers those team members to be accountable for their own measurable results, to drive their own professional development, and to help others succeed. When the team members take control of their contribution to winning, the line of sight with the principal owner is complete, with everyone accepting his share in being number one. The DNA template shapes the selection, attitudes, and development of the players and support staff (coaches and scouts). It is translated at each level and in each component of the organization. It reflects the nuances that must be incorporated into each unique staff requirement. For the Yankees and all other business organizations, the most basic element of the DNA template is the expectation of success. Players who do not accept or adapt to this expectation do not remain on the team. Those who do remain have ownership in the winning tradition.

LESSONS FOR YOUR TEAM

How to implement the "Cultivate Ownership Values from the Top Down" principle:

1. Infuse a principal owner, chief executive officer, president, or general manager with the authority to represent the legal owners.

2. Select a principal owner who possesses a willingness to be visible and involved with stakeholders inside and outside the organization.

3. Establish a clear commitment to being number one in a specific competitive environment.

4. Ensure that the principal owner establishes clear measurements and milestones for achieving ongoing success. Members of the organization must know what being number one is in their competitive environment.

5. Make sure that the principal owner establishes a clear set of values or competencies that guide the selection and ongoing behaviors of the managers and all the employees. All lower-level translations of these behaviors must reflect the owner's values.

6. Help all employees understand and believe in the core values of the organization, which are instilled by the principal owner. Empowered ownership is integral to citizenship in a winning organization.

7. Establish a direct, strong, and ongoing channel of communication between the principal owner and all members of his organization. The principal owner should meet with all new managers and should communicate periodically with all managers and employees.

Hire the Best Frontline Managers You Can Find (They're the Most Important People in Your Organization)

The field manager, or first-level manager, represents the key formal figure (frontline authority) of an organization's structure. This person is the face of the organization that each member of the team sees every day. The team's performance is heavily determined by the operational and strategic decisions made by the field manager. The field manager is the bridge from ownership and management to the players.

The first-level manager in your organization is responsible for supervising the employees who develop or sell services or products. With the authority of the owners, the first-level manager plans, organizes, and/or integrates a function or set of employee activities. The first-level manager must possess all the professional, citizenship, and leadership competencies exemplified by ownership to help your organization create and sustain excellence.

Selection of Yankee First-Level Managers

For the players and employees, the heart of every organization, first-level managers play a crucial role in instilling a winning culture and driving success. During the Yankee dynasty, the first-level managers were uniquely suited for winning with the Yankees—but not because they had outstanding prior accomplishments. On the whole, they generally had not been successful managers before arriving in New York. In fact, most had managed previous teams to sub-.500 records. But they understood things about the Yankees that others did not. They shared the values of the Yankee organization, of the owner and general manager, and instilled those values in their players. More than any other factors, their passion for winning, knowledge of the game, leadership skills, and citizenship led to their success with their new team. In this chapter, we'll examine each of these attributes of the first-level manager and why its contribution to the Yankee dynasty is invaluable.

The most successful managers of the Yankee dynasty were:

- Miller Huggins (1918–1929) and Joe McCarthy (1931–1946) under Jacob Ruppert.

- Casey Stengel (1949–1960) and Ralph Houk (1961–1963 and 1966–1973) under Larry MacPhail/Del Webb/Dan Topping.

- Joe Torre (1996–present) under current owner George Steinbrenner.

These men, who managed 60 out of the 91 teams fielded during the Yankee dynasty, shared the values of the Yankee organization. They possessed the professional skills, citizenship in the organization, and leadership skills prized by the owner and the general manager as being essential for success (Chapter 1). It was these skills more than their previous accomplishments that were held in high regard by Yankee management. Often, the selection of the field manager was controversial, with the media, the public, and even members of the organization balking at the choice. But by utilizing the set of Yankee principles as guidelines, the organization was able to make the right choice with surprising regularity, and seemingly against all odds. In this chapter, we'll look at the selection of the most representative Yankee managers during the dynasty, examine how and why they were selected, and then look at their skills and accomplishments within the organization.

Basis for Selecting a Field Manager

None of the Yankee managers had outstanding managerial records before or after their tenure with the team. Joe McCarthy, the most successful, had won a single league championship, and he was the most successful of the lot. Huggins, Stengel, and Torre had career losing records with previous teams. How did men with such little success as managers land the most prized managerial job in sports?

The Yankee managers were selected by ownership and the general manager not on the basis of prior accomplishments but rather for their potential for winning with the Yankees, their long-standing relationship with baseball, and their Yankee-compatible values. With one exception, all of these managers had exhibited grittiness as players, often overcoming physical or skill inadequacies to persevere as major leaguers, and had shown a disciplined, player-development style of managing. But above all, they had shown a passion for the game and a determination to win. They had made baseball their lives and livelihoods, and desired to be successful in the game after their playing days were over. Let's look at each manager in detail, as well as the owner responsible for hiring him.

Miller Huggins

Jacob Ruppert, the second owner of the Yankees who began the Yankee dynasty when he and Colonel Huston purchased the team in 1915, strongly believed that the manager position was the key to putting the Yankees on a winning track. Since their inception as the New York Highlanders in 1903, the Yankees had enjoyed only five winning seasons and zero trips to the postseason. Ruppert set out to change that, and he knew that he needed a field manager who would not just coach the team, but who would lead them and instill in them the Yankee principles that he believed in. Ruppert asked Ban Johnson, president of the American League, to suggest the right man for the job. Ban recommended that Ruppert sign Miller Huggins, the scrawny manager of the St. Louis Cardinals of the National League. Huggins had managed the Cardinals for five years, during which they had managed to finish last twice and no higher than third. Co-owner Colonel Huston was not impressed with the record and objected to the selection. But Ruppert had an intuitive feeling about the feisty bachelor whose life was devoted to baseball. Ruppert stood behind his managerial choice and ultimately ended his partnership with Huston over disagreements about Huggins. Huggins went on to manage the Yankees to six World Series, three of which the Yankees won.

Miller Huggins helped create and was an integral part of a model organization, which institutionalized a framework of future success. The Yankees were ahead of their time in the 1920s with a codified division of responsibility and mutual respect. The men did not interfere on each other's turf. Huggins was the field general, and management supported him in his decisions, even when it came to controlling Babe Ruth. While Huggins managed a talented team, his greatest feat was in managing Ruth. In Huggins' words, "A manager has his cards dealt to him and he must play them." One of the challenging cards was

Babe Ruth. With his unparalleled success, Ruth was becoming bigger than the game. Fans across the country loved him. The press adored him, and wrote about him constantly. But he was not an easy athlete to manage, and Huggins had to endure many disrespectful outbursts and disciplinary infractions by the Babe. But despite Ruth's success and his ability to draw fans to the stadium, Ruppert supported Huggins' decisions to fine his superstar player for rules infractions. These decisions were not easy to make but they reinforced Huggins' total authority over the team. Ruppert believed in Huggins' ability to lead the team and to make the right decisions. He knew Huggins shared his own values. This relationship set the precedent for future relationships between owners and managers, and led to unprecedented success on the field.

Joe McCarthy

In 1931, Ed Barrow hired Joe McCarthy to manage the Yankees. Babe Ruth opposed Barrow's choice. Ruth believed that he should have been named the new field manager. But Barrow stood firm in his decision and did not give in to his superstar despite pressure from Ruth's fan base and friends in the media.

Joe McCarthy's pre-Yankee record was the best of any manager of the dynasty. He had brought the National League Chicago Cubs to the World Series in 1929, and finished second with the team in 1930. Barrow admired the Philadelphia Irishman's dedication to the game, intelligence, and encyclopedic knowledge of baseball. McCarthy inherited a team that had won its division in six of the preceding 10 years, and won the World Championship three of those times. With seemingly everyone against him, including his superstar, the media, and most of the fans, McCarthy was able to win. He gained some measure of control over Babe Ruth and led the Yankees to seven World Series championships in eight appearances.

McCarthy made being a Yankee something special. He was the first Yankee manager to formally recognize the existence of Yankee tradition, and he demanded that it be maintained. McCarthy insisted that his players look and act like Yankees on and off the field, which McCarthy interpreted as wearing a coat and tie and behaving like a model citizen. The players for the most part respected McCarthy's professionalism. Joe DiMaggio called him "the best manager I ever played for."

Casey Stengel

Casey Stengel came to the Yankees in 1949 from a myriad of unsuccessful managing experiences. In 1925, after a successful career as a player, Stengel became a field manager on the Brooklyn Dodgers, a franchise that was losing games and bleeding money. Stengel could not revive the slumping franchise, and was soon back looking for a job, remarking, "Brooklyn was the borough of churches and bad ball clubs, many of which I had." Stengel next moved to another hopeless team, the Boston Braves. There he became the butt of sportswriters' and fans' jokes as he tried to clown his way through a managing fiasco. Stengel was discharged from the Braves in 1943. It appeared to most people that his major league field manager days were behind him.

But Stengel didn't quit. He took a job with a Yankee farm team in Kansas City, Missouri, and had moved up to managing the Oakland, California, team in the Pacific Coast League in 1948 when the Yankees were seeking a new field manager. George Weiss, Yankee general manager at the time, chose Stengel, who had received glowing reports for his dedication and energetic managing skills from the Yankee scouts. Weiss also was awed by Stengel's "trivia bank" on players. Weiss had a hard sell convincing the Yankee owners, Dan Topping and Del Webb, who were afraid that Stengel did not fit the Yankee image of class and dignity. Stengel had a reputation as a clown. Weiss assured them, "Casey will win with the club and he'll make money." Casey might have been a clown but he was a clown with dignity, professionalism, and sound citizenship.

Stengel managed the team for 13 seasons, a span many consider to be the most successful period of any major league franchise. The Yankees won five straight World Series, finished out of first place only twice, set new team records, and introduced the world to Mickey Mantle. Stengel lived up to Weiss' expectations, sustaining both the winning tradition and the financial integrity of the team; and he did it in his own entertaining way.

Ralph Houk

One successful manager was homegrown. Ralph Houk followed Casey Stengel as manager when Casey was forced to retire at age 70 in 1960. The press was even more critical of this dismissal than they had been of Stengel's hiring 12 years before. Stengel, too, was critical of the move. He stated, "I was fired. I'll never make the mistake of being 70 again." The owners felt it was time for a change in order to keep the team on a competitive track and turned to Houk, who had been a Yankee coach and groomed for the field manager's job by Stengel himself. Houk had a long history with the Yankees since his playing days as Yankee catcher from 1947 through 1954 and then as coach. He was steeped in Yankee tradition and trusted by the owners to uphold Yankee pride, and he was highly respected by the players. Houk had two managing stints with the Yankees, from 1961 to 1963 and from 1966 to 1973, and was the team's general manager in the intervening years. Houk was the first field manager to win the World Series in each of his first two seasons. His most successful period was 1961 through 1964.

Joe Torre

In 1996, George Steinbrenner was searching for a field manager after his perfectionist manager Buck Showalter stepped down. Showalter had helped put the Yankees into its first postseason play after 13 years of laboring in the lowlands of baseball's vineyards; but trouble lurked below the surface of his relationship with Steinbrenner. Trouble with managers was not new to the demanding Steinbrenner. His reign had been characterized by frequent managerial upheavals. Showalter was the Yankees' fifth manager in eight years and had managed the team for three seasons. But as Yogi Berra might say, it was managerial "déjà vu all over again." There was a falling-out with Steinbrenner when Showalter insisted on retaining his coaches, against Steinbrenner's wishes, following a defeat in the first round of the postseason playoffs.

Steinbrenner needed a new field manager. He was contemplating naming Joe Torre, a Brooklyn native and nine-time major league All-Star as well as former manager of the Braves, Mets, and Cardinals, to be his new manager. Steinbrenner liked Torre's quiet, dignified manner, and his success as a ballplayer. The choice was greeted with skepticism by the press and fans. Torre had never won a championship in his previous managerial tours of duty. "Clueless Joe," barked the press, a sentiment echoed by the fans. Steinbrenner, however, heeded the advice of a trusted assistant and his own intuition and hired Torre. Torre went on to manage the Yankees to a World Series win in his first year and has led them to the postseason ever since. He has four World Series rings in his jewelry collection to date.

What Made the Yankee Managers Successful?

As we've seen, the field managers of the Yankee dynasty were hired not because of their prior records, but for their passion for the game, their tenacious desire to win, and their potential for successfully managing the Yankees. In addition, all successful Yankee managers had the superior professional skills necessary to manage the team. Tommy Holmes, Boston Braves pitcher under Stengel in 1942, stated, "Casey Stengel had more baseball brains in his little finger than any other manager I knew had in their whole body." Maury Allen, sportswriter, gave Stengel credit for an additional skill that enhanced his technical skills in the perception of the baseball world: "He was a brilliant strategist and could play the press like Heifetz played the fiddle." Let's now look at the specific competencies that set these first-level managers apart.

Professional Skills

Stellar professional skills are the foundation for a field manager's success. Joe McCarthy was adept at putting together an offense. He was an innovator who enhanced his team's offensive output through novel strategies. He was the first manager to understand the importance of hitters' taking pitches, working the count to their advantage so that the pitcher would be pressured into throwing a hittable pitch. He also recognized the value of a balanced team of both scrappy, nimble players who punch the ball and get on base through their quickness and power hitters who swing for the fences. McCarthy was the first manager to divide a pitching staff into starters and relievers. In 1936, he assigned his pitchers definitive roles in the rotation or the bullpen.

Casey Stengel earned the nickname "The Old Perfessor" for his brilliant field managing strategies. He maximized the abilities of his players for the benefit of the team by utilizing a platoon system in which he would have several players assigned to each field position. He recognized the value of bench strength and assigned players based on the situation. If a position player went into a batting slump, Stengel was quick to replace even a star with a backup. Stengel also understood the advantage of maximizing his team's double-play advantage. He avoided putting two right-handed sluggers back-to-back in the lineup because that type of batter is vulnerable to hitting into double plays. He preferred pitchers who induced batters to hit ground balls, increasing the possibility of turning a double play, and he liked batters who hit fly balls, avoiding the double play possibility. Stengel's Yankee teams had large advantages over their opponents in double plays. The year before Stengel became manager the Yankees turned 161 double plays and their hitters grounded into 136. Under Stengel the positive ratio for double plays increased dramatically. From a plus 25 before Stengel's managing tenure, the positive advantage went to 54 during his first year, 66 his second, and 112 in his fifth year.

Let's look at additional professional skills that the managers of the Yankee dynasty possessed in addition to being outstanding strategists.

- *Talent management.* Not every winning Yankee team was composed of a preponderance of superstar and star players. The 1998 team under Joe Torre is an example of a savvy manager reaching success by recognizing that the whole is greater than the sum of its parts. The representative Yankee managers, listed earlier, knew how to select players, where they fit, and when and how to use them. They established an atmosphere where the players knew that the team came first and that the manager could make them a winner. The players knew that the manager would extract optimal performance from all players.

- *Straight communication.* All managers were honest and open with their players, leading to respectful and trusting relationships. Clear and open communications facilitated the players' support for the manager's tactical and operational decisions.

- *Knowledge management.* Yankee managers excelled at selection and coordination of a cohesive, skilled coaching staff. The coaches are the content, strategic, and operational experts who are essential to maximizing team performance. The coaches help assure the continual assessment and development of the players based on a constantly evolving set of organizational needs and standards. They also supply additional analysis and interpretation of ongoing activities necessary for high-quality decisions.

- *Strategic management.* Whether they did it intuitively or formally, the best of the Yankee managers were able to develop and implement a clear game plan. They were quite familiar with the strengths and weaknesses of their competitors and how to address them in a fluid set of conditions.

- *Risk taking.* The Yankees would not have succeeded unless the managers took calculated risks. They were certainly not afraid to make important decisions based on limited information but with good intuitive sense.

- *Superstar counseling.* All Yankee managers recognized that they had to build their team around a superstar. They correctly emphasized this category of player and focused on cultivating superstars' contributions.

- *Game management.* No manager is successful without a profound understanding of the official rules of the game and the ability to use the rules to advantage. This includes knowing the strengths and weaknesses of each competitive venue.

- *Crisis management.* Sound decision making in times of crisis has been a hallmark of the dynasty. Successful decision making at critical moments is essential both to winning games and to earning the respect of players and senior management. For example, Casey Stengel started a journeyman pitcher named Don Larsen in the fifth game of the 1956 World Series after a poor performance in the second game. Larsen proceeded to pitch the only perfect game in World Series history. Stengel relied on his knowledge of the game, intuition, and risk taking to make baseball history.

- *Perseverance.* The managers never lost sight of the team goal of winning.

Citizenship

Outstanding managers are role models for their players. They exemplify the behaviors and values that enable a team to function as a cohesive unit. Eddie Lopat, Yankee pitcher, said of Stengel, "If there was any one great skill Casey had as a manager, it was knowing when to pick his spots. He didn't have a degree, but he was one of the greatest doctors of psychiatry I had ever seen." Stengel was also respected for his ability to incorporate the first Yankee black players into the team. Elston Howard, one of these first black Yankees, said of Stengel, "He made me feel part of the club. He made me feel like a Yankee."

Let's look at the specific citizenship skills that the managers of the Yankee dynasty possessed.

- *Loyalty to ownership.* Sometimes strong personalities that share many common characteristics do not mesh. The most successful managers were able to adapt to demanding owners for long periods of time. Managers who could not adapt did not last long. The successful managers were able to modify their styles to those of the owners.

- *Keeper of the Yankee flame.* The successful managers understood their role in the perpetuation of the Yankee mystique. They instilled in their players an awareness of the Yankee Way by socializing the players, coaches, and other staff members in the traditional Yankee values. The managers made new team members feel welcome and oriented them to the team's winning traditions and culture.

- *Ownership filter.* Yankee managers acted as the direct liaison between the front office and players by clearly communicating ownership goals and vision.

- *Evenhandedness.* The successful managers treated players, fans, media, and other constituents with fairness and respect.

Leadership

When speaking of Miller Huggins, Mark Koenig, one of Huggins' solid role players, stated, "He made you feel like a giant." Huggins exemplified the leadership qualities that maximized the potential of all his players. Don Zimmer, Yankee coach, summed up Joe Torre's quiet leadership: "Joe lets players play and coaches coach." Torre's leadership skills are recognized and admired by his players. Darryl Strawberry, Yankee outfielder from 1995 to 1999, said of Torre, "His impact is all over this team. It's all over every player." Andy Pettitte, Yankee pitcher from 1995 to 2003, praised Torre with the words, "I think Skip's the kind of guy who's going to go down with the guys that got him here. As a player you love that."

Let's look at the specific leadership qualities that the managers of the Yankee dynasty possessed.

- *Optimistic.* Casey Stengel joked his way through trying times with flip one-liners and jovial banter. Joe Torre looks for a positive slant to all situations. All the managers looked for the up side even in negative situations.

- *Composed.* Successful Yankee managers stay calm under trying conditions and maintain equilibrium during setbacks. Torre remains consistently stoic and reflective under good as well as poor conditions. Stengel was a jester, preferring to take the heat off his players through comic gestures and eccentric language. Huggins rationalized and structured events to take away the uncertainty. McCarthy remained stoic and unruffled through the most trying times with Babe Ruth and refused to allow Ruth to upset team equilibrium. The styles were different but the goal was the same.

- *Innovative.* Every Yankee manager was innovative in a significant way. They used their own novel ideas or leveraged those of others to reach success. McCarthy formalized the use of a system for using starting pitchers called the "rotation." This was based on his assessment of the optimal intervals between pitching assignments necessary to capture as frequently as possible the capabilities of his best pitchers. Stengel formally introduced "platooning." This was a method for utilizing his pitchers and hitters opposite to the strength of the opposing player (Stengel's right-handed hitter against an opponent's left-handed pitcher, Stengel's left-handed pitcher versus an opponent's left-handed hitter). These innovations forced major strategic and operational decisions on the part of the competition.

- *Clear*. The managers always demanded performance levels that at least equaled their assessment of the player's capabilities. They also communicate expected citizenship and leadership behaviors. Stengel once reprimanded superstar Mickey Mantle for not giving his complete effort in hustling out a ground ball. Mantle now clearly understood Stengel's expectations.

- *Mature*. Every successful manager in the Yankee dynasty was over 50 years of age when selected and had gained diverse experience at many baseball venues and levels. They also had observed many players and managers and had the opportunity to recognize what behaviors made them successful.

- *Humble*. The managers knew that the players were the principal reasons for success. Casey Stengel, when asked why he was successful, said, "I couldna' done it without my players."

- *Catalytic*. The successful managers found and developed other leaders. They identified and reinforced players and coaches who were able to constructively support, and influence others to support the values, behaviors, skills, and management style of the team.

On a few occasions, principal owners selected managers who were lacking in key characteristics. The most notorious of these managers was Billy Martin. Martin had an excellent knowledge of the tactics and strategies of the game, was a good judge of talent and how to allocate it, and had a passion for winning, but he was immature, lacked critical skills in citizenship, failed to support the principal owner, and was a divisive leader of his players. The result of his selection was disruption and chaos within the organization, and it contributed to the second dark age, the period of 1982–1995, when the Yankees did not reach the World Series.

First-Level Manager: Your Key to Success

The first-level manager is a major key to organization success. This person is the organizational face the employees see every day. First-level managers must be selected on the basis that they will represent ownership expectations and ideals in a clear and fair manner. They must possess all the professional, citizenship, and leadership competencies to help your organization create and sustain excellence. No manager should stay in that position unless he or she embraces the characteristics of the principal owner.

LESSONS FOR YOUR TEAM

How to implement the "Hire the Best Frontline Managers You Can Find" principle:

1. Select first-level managers who reflect the values and expectations of the principal owner. This means translating the characteristics prized by the principal owner into success criteria for the manager, and getting multiple assessors to arrive at a selection decision. The decision may not be unanimous, but it must be based on competency assessment.

2. Don't be afraid to weigh values and competencies ahead of prior accomplishments and reputation in selecting first-level managers.

3. First-level managers must add value to the success of the organization. They must bring a blend of professional, leadership, and citizenship skills that are in line with required organizational competencies.

4. First-level managers must be empowered to do their jobs with input from ownership and management but without their interference.

CHAPTER

3

Formally Recognize Your Informal Leaders

Every company or team should have formally recognized team leaders. They are the individuals who excel at their jobs, who inspire others to excel, and who display behaviors that bring credit to the team. They are first recognized and respected as leaders by their teammates. Organizations must acknowledge and support these leaders. In baseball, this person is designated captain. The captain is a role model who links traditional winning ways to current conditions. This chapter looks at the Yankee captains' important characteristics, examines the role these men played on their team, and looks at the role of the captain in a modern business setting.

Yankee Team Captains

There were eight Yankee captains between 1922 and 2004. They were officially designated captain for four reasons:

1. Their accomplishments exceeded the accomplishments of their peers.

2. They inspired others to superior performance.

3. They embodied the core values of the organization.

4. They were recognized and respected as team leaders by their teammates.

Players needed to fulfill all four of these requirements before management would bestow the title of captain. At times, there was no Yankee captain as no player on the team at the time lived up to the role. The most inspiring of the team captains are Lou Gehrig, Thurman Munson, Don Mattingly, and Derek Jeter, the current captain. Let's look at each of these men individually.

Lou Gehrig

Although Lou Gehrig died more than 60 years ago, he is still revered as the model for all succeeding captains and for all players. Gehrig's excellence on and off the field is the benchmark for superior accomplishments, high levels of performance, stellar citizenship, and quiet leadership. He stands as a symbol and benchmark for Yankee excellence and core values.

Gehrig's numbers in his 16-year career are legendary, and if his career had not been cut short by illness, many of his records would remain unbroken. Compared to even current superstars, Gehrig's statistics are incredibly impressive. He is most remembered for his consecutive games played streak of 2,130 games, which ended in 1939 when he voluntarily requested to be removed "for the good of the team." He was called "The Iron Horse" for his determination and persistence. In 1927, despite Ruth's home run record set that year, Gehrig was voted the American League's Most Valuable Player. That honor was earned for his leadership and citizenship in addition to his hitting and other professional skills.

Statistics made Gehrig a superstar. However, his value to his team went far beyond mere numbers. His work ethic set an example for his younger teammates. He would arrive at the ballpark early to practice and was always open to coaching suggestions and constructive criticism in order to help his team win. He played through pain without complaint. He did not seek honors and was content to take a backseat to first Babe Ruth and then Joe DiMaggio. He just wanted to be the ultimate professional at his job. Gehrig made the team come first.

So revered was Gehrig that the Yankees made no official designation of captain between his death in 1941 and Thurman Munson's elevation to that role in 1976. It was said that the ghost of the deceased Iron Horse continued to be the Yankee spiritual captain during that period.

Thurman Munson

Thurman Munson was the Yankee catcher in the 1970s. He was an outstanding player among a team of consummate professionals. Munson was respected for his intensity, resolve, and constant demand for excellence, both of himself and of his teammates. Chris Chambliss, Yankee first baseman and Munson's teammate, said, "He told me where I should play this hitter, told the center fielder where he should play, and communicated with the pitcher besides. A lot of guys looked up to Thurman's hard-nosed kind of play. With him, you just thought you were going to win." In 1976, the same year he was honored as the Most Valuable Player of the American League, Munson was appointed captain. That year, the Yankees won their first pennant in 12 years. Munson was the catcher during the Yankee World Series victories in 1977 and 1978.

Munson's batting accomplishments were most impressive, but Munson was more than just a talented hitter. He won three Gold Gloves for his catching skills.

Munson wanted to win every game. In the early 1970s, when the Yankees were hopelessly fighting to finish in the middle of the pack, Munson showed the same intensity as he later would in postseason championship games. He took every loss as a personal affront. He would practice for hours before each game and stay after the game to further hone his skills. He would run the bases with abandon, hustling to turn a double into a triple. In one game he was beaned twice and then was spiked at home plate. The injury required several stitches, but rather than be replaced, Munson insisted on returning to the field and finishing the game.

Munson's citizenship was revealed in quiet ways. He would visit sick children in hospitals without letting anyone know. He never sought accolades from his club or the media. He led by example. He was admired and respected by his teammates and the fans.

Don Mattingly

Don Mattingly first played for the Yankees in 1982, a year after they appeared in the World Series, and retired in 1995, a year before the Yankees played in their next fall classic. During his Yankee tenure, Mattingly compiled impressive batting statistics. He also won nine Gold Glove awards (for defensive ability) and a Most Valuable Player plaque. Mattingly was considered the best fielding first baseman in Yankee history and was nicknamed "Donnie Baseball" as recognition of his love for and dedication to the game. He stated, "I love playing the game. That's what I'm here for." He yearned to win and, when his team struggled, he worked even harder at developing his skills and inspiring his teammates.

No player has ever played in as many games for the Yankees without winning a World Championship as Mattingly. Yet Paul O'Neill, Yankee outfielder in the 1990s, among countless others, credited Mattingly with setting the tone that later resulted in championships. O'Neill stated, "Ten or 20 years down the road, people will always associate Don Mattingly with the Yankees. There are a few guys who, whether you're playing with them or against them, you root for them. He is one of those guys. People in baseball wanted Donnie to do well because of all he'd done and how he had done it."

Mattingly is another Yankee who led quietly by example. Mattingly stated, "I always wanted to keep it strictly baseball. When the fans thought about me, they thought about baseball, not about a commercial or about a celebrity or anything like that." He always presented himself as a professional baseball player and, since his retirement, has devoted himself to coaching other players. In 2004 he became a Yankee hitting coach under Joe Torre.

Derek Jeter

Derek Jeter came to the Yankees in 1996, won Rookie of the Year honors, and, like his predecessor captains, has left his mark in a low-key, unassuming manner. Since he is still playing, final statistics are not part of his bio, but he is the acknowledged indispensable man on his team. In 2000, Jeter became the first player to win both the All-Star Game and World Series Most Valuable Player awards. He is an athlete of grace, talent, and maturity who does not let his desire to win get in the way of good sportsmanship. He is admired and respected by diverse members of the organization and community, including the owner, his teammates, media, and fans both young and old. He has coped with the demands imposed on New York celebrities with maturity. Joe Torre, his manager, states, "He's more than just a talented kid. He's a good kid who has his priorities straight." Basketball legend Michael Jordan says of Jeter, "I love his work ethic. He has a great attitude. He has the qualities that separate superstars from everyday people."

Jeter once said, "All I ever wanted to be is a Yankee. When I was a kid, I was always hoping there's a jersey left for me to wear with a single digit, because of all the retired numbers." Jeter wears number 2 with Yankee pride and states he wishes to wear it for his whole baseball career.

Among his teammates, Jeter is regarded as a perpetually upbeat guy with no conceit. His teammates feed on his positive outlook and quiet leadership. His teammates emulate his example. However, his good-natured approach does not interfere with his concentration or performance on the field.

Jeter understands his obligations to his team and to fans. He consistently behaves politely and with poise. He is a role model for other players and his young fans.

Homegrown Talent

Lou Gehrig, Thurman Munson, Don Mattingly, and Derek Jeter, all Yankee captains, came through the Yankee farm system. They were not traded for or bought from other teams. These men had absorbed the principles and values of the organization early in their careers. Highly skillful scouts identified their budding talent and potential for superior performance and brought them into the Yankee organization. In the farm system, their skills were developed and they became enmeshed in the Yankee culture. In the minor leagues, managers and coaches imparted Yankee pride in addition to professional skills.

All the captains had quality professional skills, and most excelled at their defensive positions as well as at the plate. All have gained the respect of ownership, management, other players, and fans, through making ongoing significant contributions to the team. All the cited captains achieved recognition by Major League Baseball by receiving Most Valuable Player awards. Both Munson's and Jeter's exceptional talents were recognized early in their careers through Rookie of the Year honors. Every Yankee captain exhibited a consistent work ethic through persistence, self-discipline, determination to improve, and willingness to accept and give coaching. They are all role models for Yankee pride.

Not All Superstars Are Captains

Some Yankee superstars never became captains. It was said that Joe DiMaggio was an inwardly focused hero with little interest in helping other players. Mickey Mantle had to learn to control his own behavior before he could guide others. Babe Ruth actually served as captain for about five days in 1922. He was relieved of this role when he behaved like his nicknames, "Baby" Ruth and the "Bambino," and not in the image of a leader. He was an iconic, immature talent who left a lasting legacy on his sport but challenged authority and created havoc within his team. Ruth was a beloved but flawed superstar who did not meet all four criteria of the captain.

Role of the Captain

As with Gehrig, Munson, Mattingly, and Jeter, the organization names a player captain when he undeniably exhibits the characteristics of a captain for some period of time and those characteristics are acknowledged by the player's teammates. Being named captain is an honor that carries much responsibility. It is an indication to the team and public that this individual has earned a significant team role and symbolizes the ideal player.

As on a ship, the captain guides the team in the right direction and makes adjustments when needed. All players are expected to reflect the prototypical characteristics of the captain at some level. As we've seen in the descriptions of the Yankee captains, there are many shared characteristics. Let's look at these shared characteristics.

Accomplishments

Captains are recognized for the following contributions:

- A high level of demonstrated accomplishments. Specifically, this means that, based on hard statistics compared to competitive players on other teams (external measure) and to overall level of relative contribution to his own team (internal measure), the captain is peerless.

- Contribution in crisis situations. The captain has demonstrated specific achievements that lead to winning in periods of crisis or while under pressure. His specific contributions are legendary and have become part of the mythology and folklore of the team.

- Knowledge of, respect for, and transmission of the winning tradition to teammates, fans, and media.

Professional Skills

Captains demonstrate the following abilities:

- A strong knowledge of the professional skills or tools of their positions.
- A willingness to work hard to improve skills and to help others improve their skills. Captains practice on their own, encourage others to practice, and will lead practice sessions.
- Willingness to seek coaches (inside) and mentors (outside) who can enhance their talents.
- A good knowledge of the rules of the game.
- Determination to exceed the skills of competitive players.
- Resolve to remain current on new ways to approach job skills and the game.

Citizenship

Captains exhibit the following traits:

- Willingness to make sacrifices for the team. When Gehrig took himself out of the lineup, he told the manager, "It was for the good of the team."
- Promotion of good relationships among teammates.
- Respect for and support of management. The captain facilitates good relationships between players and management.

- Recognition of the importance of image with the fans and media.

- Treatment of fans and media with unconditional respect. The captain makes himself available to fans and media.

- Intensity and commitment to achieving winning on-field results.

- Proper preparation to play hard and to play through injuries or illness. Gehrig played through debilitating illness until he could no longer perform to his already high standards.

- Exemplary manners.

- Dignified conduct.

- An aura of quiet pride in a job well done.

Leadership

Captains lead by the following actions:

- Seizing opportunities to succeed in clutch situations. The captain desires to excel for the benefit of the team over individual accomplishments.

- Engendering trust from management and other players.

- Gaining respect of other players. Players are proud to be his teammate and like him as a person.

- Showing respect for other players and treating everyone equally and fairly.

- Offering and being sought for advice and counsel by teammates.

- Inspiring other players to play to their optimal abilities.

- Exhibiting poise, self-control, and confidence.

- Communicating well with management and teammates.

- Demonstrating consistently sound judgment and thoughtful decisions.

- Helping attract needed talent to the team.

As we come to the end of the first part of this book, the leadership structure for a successful organization is now clear. The principal owner sets the values for the organization that are embodied by the field manager and captain and passed throughout the organization. With these three pillars of the organization in place, you have a foundation for success.

Who are the heroes and role models in your organization? Who are the people who deliver in the clutch? Every organization must find, cultivate, and recognize their captains.

LESSONS FOR YOUR TEAM

How to implement the "Formally Recognize Your Informal Leaders" principle:

1. Make explicit the behaviors expected for members of your organization. The organization should seek to attract, develop, and retain people who have these behaviors. From these, leaders will emerge who embody your organizational competencies.

2. Look for the early emergence of "captains." Everyone is expected to be a leader at some level. Many of the Yankee captains emerged from their demonstration of positive influence on others, their superior professional skills, and outstanding citizenship while in the farm system.

(Continued)

LESSONS FOR YOUR TEAM *(Continued)*

3. Remember that leaders are anointed and not appointed. They are recognized by fellow employees as outstanding workers, great people, and role models for the organization's values. They are respected, revered, and emulated.

4. Formally recognize leaders who demonstrate specific behaviors that reinforce the goal of achieving competitive supremacy and that support the values of the organization. Some possibilities are:

- Assigning them as mentors to junior employees.

- Appointing them to head task forces.

- Putting them in charge of projects.

- Assigning them as team leaders.

- Having them facilitate important meetings.

- Letting them solve special organization problems.

- Publicly recognizing them in publications and other media.

- Providing contact with the principal owner.

PART II

Processes for Developing and Maintaining a Dynasty

CHAPTER

4

Set the Bar Higher Than Your People Have Ever Seen It: Quantitative Performance Measures

Every organization must have clear and established winning standards for the organization as a whole, and for each employee. Everyone must be clear as to what constitutes winning. For the Yankees, winning is equated with a World Championship. To repeatedly achieve this lofty goal, all Yankee players must accept that specific measures of individual accomplishment are subordinate to winning the World Series. Expectations for player performance will be high, concrete, and linked to the team goal. For the organization and the players the measures must be unequivocal.

Yankee team success is also measured by the size of the fan base relative to other baseball and sports teams. The owner's goal is to sell out the ballpark and to dominate the airwaves. Success is also equated with the variety and numbers of Yankee products sold in a multitude of outlets. The size of the fan base is the foundation for financial competitive advantage, which in turn translates into increased ability to reinvest in the team by securing and paying for the best available talent, which ultimately results in additional fans. The Yankee goal is to put the most competitive team on the field not only to win

*championships but to attract and retain the greatest number of fans. In the
corporate world, the fan base is akin to the customer pool.*

*Often, an organization will compare itself to another organization,
identifying that organization as its main competition. For any organization this
means knowing the strengths, weaknesses, and success potential of the closest
competitor and using these parameters to stimulate a spirited rivalry. This
chapter looks at the high bar the Yankees have set for themselves throughout
the dynasty, the definition of success at the organizational and individual levels, and the effect that having a competitive foil has had on Yankee success.*

Quantitative Performance Measures Are Baseball's Legacy

Baseball blazed a trail in the use of "hard" performance measures. It
would be difficult to find another institution that has developed such a
meticulous accounting of its accomplishments. On October 22, 1845,
the first set of individual and team performance measurements was reported in the *New York Morning News*. This "box score" was produced
only one month after Alexander Cartwright and his Knickerbocker
teammates established the rules of baseball. Since 1871, according to
Total Baseball, 6th Edition, more than 170,000 games played by over
15,000 players exceeding 2,300 team seasons have been recorded. With
baseball's evolution, the types of performance measures have increased
in number and complexity. The manipulation of accomplishment measures, however, has been made considerably easier by the introduction
of the computer. Statistics are readily available to every stakeholder on
every conceivable aspect of the game. The computer has also enhanced
baseball's ability to link player contribution to team success.

Baseball, from the beginning of its hazy origins, was also a pio-
neer in the use of benchmarking. The more savvy and disciplined

owners and executives were able to use comparative statistics to make better decisions on player acquisition, retention, positioning, and pay. While it is unclear as to the degree to which owners Ruppert, Topping and Webb, and Steinbrenner actually applied such sophisticated approaches (performance measures, databases, benchmarking) to their nonbaseball businesses, they were highly proficient in using them with the Yankees.

Although performance measurements have been part of the baseball landscape for more than 150 years, the manipulation of this data was rudimentary and intuitive for much of baseball's history. The Yankees, however, were particularly skillful in their application of available data even before computers allowed for sophisticated analyses. For example, in the precomputer era, manager Casey Stengel was widely recognized for the most efficient utilization of his reserve players as measured by the statistic known as "bench value percentage." In a corporate environment this measure would relate to the maximization of all employees' skills in achieving successful organization results.

Today the Yankees, and their competitors, use a wide array of respected statistical sources. These sources are the business analogue of industry, professional, research, quality, and productivity associations. These baseball sources include Elias Sports Bureau, *Total Baseball*, and the Society for American Baseball Research. These and other sources provide the Yankees with input for their computer simulations. These simulations, in turn, provide not only talent management data but information necessary to make tactical game decisions. For example: A manager retrieves data on his batters' accomplishments versus an opponent's pitcher and how to align players in the field based on batter hitting tendencies.

Hard data on accomplishments and their associated contexts are used by all baseball teams. Next time you watch a baseball game notice the book with the computer printout used by the managers and coaches to bring hard measures of player accomplishments and prospective tendencies to the field decision-making process. It is the effective application of this information over time that separates the Yankees from other teams. Yankee managers and coaching staffs have been adept at balancing accomplishment data with Yankee professional, citizenship, and leadership skills to maximize player output and convert competitive information into a recipe for winning.

Team Success: Set the Bar High

It has often been said that people behave as they are measured. In 1920, Babe Ruth's first full year with the Yankees, the team failed to win the league title. Although the Yankees' attendance swelled that year due in part to Ruth's presence, and profits increased dramatically, owner Jacob Ruppert was not satisfied. Increased profits were obviously appreciated, and the team performed better than they had in the previous year, but such success was not what Ruppert was pursuing.

In 1921 and 1922 the Yankees won league titles, but lost the World Series. Again Ruppert was pleased with the increased performance of his team and manager, but he had set his sights on a World Championship. In 1923, the Yankees won the World Series—but Ruppert was still not content: The next year he expected an even more dominant season. Winning the World Championship was the primary measure of success for the organization, and it remains so today. The bar had been set at the highest possible level, and the Yankee dynasty was built on this definition of success.

Winning the World Championship is the organizational goal. Everything else, including all levels of individual accomplishment, comes after this goal. Monumental struggles have been waged between ownership, management, and players who did not understand or accept this basic principle of the Yankee team doctrine. Even superstar players like Babe Ruth and Reggie Jackson were ultimately challenged to toe the line and put the team before personal feats. Ruth challenged Ruppert and Miller Huggins, his manager, with his rebellious antics. Reggie Jackson challenged the authority of George Steinbrenner and his manager, Billy Martin. The ultimate result of these confrontations was always the same. The owner supported the manager in putting team concerns before the superstar's ego, and finally, through admonishments, fines, ultimatums, and suspensions, the players were forced, unwillingly, to modify their behaviors. Players who do not accept the clear doctrine of "the team comes first" are finally traded or simply dropped. There is no compromise.

Joe Williams, a reporter, recognized the manager's need to enforce the Yankee doctrine of "the team comes first" when he wrote in the *New York World Telegram* in the 1920s: "I know of no one who could have taken over a bunch of artificial prima donnas such as was handed to Miller Huggins when he first came to New York and turned them ultimately into a perfect machine-like organism." The owner's expectation is explicit: Take outstanding players with different self-interests and personal agendas and transform them into a team working as one entity to achieve the designated organizational goal of finishing first. Historically, there have been many teams with superstar players who have never achieved the sustained success of the Yankees because they never understood the need to measure the superstar's performance on the basis of his contribution to the team rather than his individual results. Personal statistics by themselves do not reflect the true nature of a player's contribution.

About 30 years after Ruppert and Huggins clearly communicated team winning as a priority over individual glory, Eddie Lopat, a Yankee pitcher under manager Casey Stengel, said, "The thing a lot of people forget about our Yankee teams is we were together. We didn't play for individual records. We played for winning." Casey Stengel once indicated that he wasn't concerned with player statistics because the Yankees paid him "to win two out of every three games."

About 50 years later, Joe Torre, manager of the 2000 World Champion Yankees, said after the final championship game, "We may not have the best players, but we certainly have the best team. What I probably most admire and am most proud of with this team is their resolve and grittiness." The bar has never been lowered, and team expectations for success permeate the whole operation. All other measures of success are matched against this one organizational goal.

Set the Bar at the Appropriate Height

"Wee Willie" Keeler, who played for the Yankees in the early years of the twentieth century, once remarked that he could help his team win by hitting singles. His legendary successful approach to achieving his goal was captured in his famous quote "I hit 'em where they ain't." Babe Ruth once bellowed that if he were paid to hit singles he would bat .600. His approach was to hit 'em way beyond where they ain't. Derek Jeter's more contemporary view is that it's the game-winning plays that are most important in measuring a player's accomplishments. His intellectual approach is based on knowing how to best respond to the critical situation at hand. Each of these three players had a personal achievement goal and a philosophy for reaching it. History has proven that each of these players was successful in linking his achievements to his goals.

A team, however, cannot wait for history to make the connection between players' goals and their methods for achieving them. It was natural, therefore, that over the course of their 80-plus-year dynasty the Yankees, as did their competitors, evolved a set of intuitive guidelines for setting expectations for player goals. These guidelines help players focus on those accomplishments that the team's management believes correlate with winning championships. These accomplishments are often reflected in the details of player contracts that frequently are unrevealed to the public and the media. It is common that the different special interest groups have different perceptions of player success. This situation leads to some spirited discussions about the worth of a player since, unlike performance measurements in the nonbaseball business world, the accomplishments of players are transparent to anyone with an interest in uncovering them. Anyone can become baseball savvy by using the extensive and readily available performance statistics on the Internet.

Criteria for Developing Performance Expectations

In general, the intuitive survival test for establishing a player's performance expectations includes the following elements:

- *Appropriateness*. The measure should relate to the specific role of the player (e.g., the lead-off hitter's on-base average and the cleanup hitter's runs batted in).
- *Criticality*. The measure must be clearly linked to winning (e.g., game-winning hits, winning runs scored, advancement of base runners, pitching performance against competitors with superior batting prowess).
- *Specificity*. The measure should tie to the accomplishment level of others in comparable roles and/or the previous achievement level of the player (e.g., the player's on-base percentage as

compared to that of the closest rival and/or previous year's performance, player's hits with runners in scoring position as compared to closest rival and/or previous year's performance.

- *Multimeasurement.* Players' contributions must be judged on several hard performance expectations (e.g., fielding and hitting percentages as compared to a benchmarked group of players).

- *Credibility.* Team management and all players accept the measurement as accurate and equitable (e.g., team management and players agree that advancing base runners correlates with team wins and that all players should be measured on this dimension).

Expectations that survive these tests can be used to establish the validity of the professional, leadership, and citizenship competencies outlined in the next chapter. The composite framework just described is a useful tool to anyone constructing performance expectations for themselves and others.

Individual Success: Set the Bar High

All standards of individual success are defined in terms of contribution to overall team achievement. Contributions to winning can be viewed on three levels: dimensions, measures, and standards. For example, for many players, one dimension would be hitting. The measure of the dimension might be batting average or home runs. The standard or level of accomplishment would be batting average or home runs compared to all players in comparable positions on other teams, and/or the top 25 of all players on all teams, and/or the top three players on the same team.

Achievements against these benchmarks will be one measure of contribution to team success. This process focuses the player on the competitors in their positions on other teams and also on a comparison of contribution to team success with players on their own teams. This is constructive competition. However, the individual success factors are always subordinated to the team goal of sustained winning and excellence.

In baseball, all teams use the same dimensions but vary on some of the measures of performance. For example, the team management may go beyond the basics of overall batting average to batting average in the clutch or crisis. Tommy Henrich, one of the Yankees' solid players, was called "Old Reliable" because of his great ability to deliver in the clutch. A long line of other players including Hank Bauer, Lou Pinella, and Paul O'Neill were not superstars but they were revered because of their ability to produce when it counted. Derek Jeter, a superstar, has contributed in the most critical of situations. Clutch hitting and pitching can be viewed as critical measures. All players must be selected, developed, and rewarded on the basis of these tough critical measures.

The critical measures are developed by the team based on a rough set of perceived statistical linkages to winning games. The ability of a team to identify, select, and cultivate people against these measures changes the competitive behaviors of the players. A player who leads the league in home runs is not as valuable as the player who hits more home runs that win games. A player who has a higher on-base average may be more valuable than one who has a higher batting average. Casey Stengel built a winning team based on hitters who did not hit into double plays, a seemingly innocuous statistic. He looked for players who had speed, gave great effort when running the bases, and were selective when swinging the bat. This was a very sophisticated perspective on hitting. Organizations that can find and apply concrete, team-success-linked, critical performance measures to the selection assessment and development of employees have a better chance of attaining competitive success.

Not every position, and therefore player, is expected to make the same level of contribution. For example, a second baseman is usually not expected to hit as many home runs as an outfielder or a designated hitter. But the minimal standard set for each team member should be higher than a peer group and sufficient to contribute to the organization's success. Not every player can be a superstar, but every player can contribute to making their team a superperforming team if they at least meet high-level expectations for their position. Exceeding individual standards becomes a source of pride and tradition for the entire organization, but it is mandatory that each employee's specific expectations of success be linked to organizational expectations for achieving number one status.

Winning Leads to More Winning

In addition to winning on the field, each Yankee team is expected to be great sports entertainment. The Yankee goal is to attract the broadest and deepest audience to their games, dominate television baseball viewers, and sell their merchandise in diverse markets. Typically, ownership measures success through relative ratings of the quality or value perceived by their fans, compared to other baseball teams, and teams in other sports. The size of the fan base compared to competitive organizations and the quality and diversity of the fan base itself are prime ownership concerns. These measures are reflected in ticket (product) sales (numbers and price), amount and value of team merchandise purchased, size of the radio and television audience, amount and value of advertising, and amount and value of player endorsements.

The Yankees reaped the financial benefits of team superiority early in the dynasty. In 1920 the Yankees were the first club to draw one million fans at home although they were still playing at the Polo Grounds, and they notched five more million-plus seasons before any other team reached that level. The Yankees broke the two million mark for five straight years after World War II. In the age of television, the Yankees have maintained their financial dominance of the rest of the major league teams with a monster cable contract. In 2004 the Yankees reached one million in paid attendance before midseason; sellouts even during midweek are a common occurrence. Such a steady revenue flow has contributed to the organization's ability to offer highly competitive pay packages to targeted players.

Defeating a Hated Enemy Is a Hard Success Measure

Most people believe that the Yankees' principal enemy was always the Boston Red Sox. They believe that intense Yankee rivalry began with the acquisition of Babe Ruth by the Yankees; this is another myth. The first venom was spewed when the Yankees moved from Baltimore (the Orioles) to New York in 1903 and became the Highlanders. The legendary John J. McGraw, manager of the National League New York Giants, had left the American League Orioles under questionable circumstances (ethics and rowdy behavior among other charges) just a short time before and his actions ultimately precipitated the team's move to New York. The Giants and the Highlanders played in different ballparks until 1913. Despite a history of antagonism, the Highlanders became the Giants' tenants that year and the level of hatred increased because, added to McGraw's transgressions, both teams knew they were competing for fans. Sometime around 1913, the Highlanders became the Yankees, but they were the "inept Yankees" while the Giants were the apple of the eye of the Big Apple.

In 1920 Babe Ruth came to the Yankees from the Boston Red Sox. This single move changed the competitive environment for the Yankees, Giants, and Red Sox. The seeds of the Yankee dynasty and Red Sox ineptitude were sown. The Giants now had a same-city force to reckon with. The Giants met the Yankees in the 1921 and 1922 World Series. Fans need only take the same subway line to all games, for games were exclusively played in the Polo Grounds, the two teams' shared ballpark. The Giants won both World Series and evicted the Yankees from the Polo Grounds. This led to the building of Yankee Stadium, also known as "The House that Ruth Built." Jacob Ruppert, principal Yankee owner, once remarked that Yankee Stadium was "the greatest mistake the Giants ever made." In 1923, the Yankees beat the Giants, to win their first World Series. The Yankees had earned baseball's exalted trophy and won the battle for New York fans. They were simultaneously despised by the Giants, the Red Sox, and the loyal fans of those clubs.

The intense rivalry with the Red Sox still exists. It has been described as Avis versus Hertz with the Red Sox "trying harder" to attain the number-one position. Since the 1920s the Red Sox have consistently finished behind their top adversary. The intensity of the teams each time they meet is surpassed only by the fervor of the fans in the stands. The media has done its part in increasing the passion. An excerpt from an article written in 2003 in the *Journal News*, a Westchester County, New York, newspaper, recounts some of the passion generated by fans, players, and the media. John Delcos writes,

> It's a rivalry that runs deep and personal, and unmatched in tenseness on the field and lore off it. Derek Jeter once lunched in Boston and

spelled out in pepperoni on his pizza was the name "Pedro," referring to Red Sox pitcher Pedro Martinez. When asked what aspect of the rivalry he enjoys most, Jeter, forever on the listening end of a running dialogue with Fenway fans when on the on-deck circle, simply said: "Beating them." "I don't have any sympathy for them. They don't have any sympathy for us."

Jeter's words echo sentiments spoken by Jacob Ruppert in the 1920s. Ruppert declared, "There is no charity in baseball."

Even though the Red Sox won the World Series in 2004 and finally eradicated the Curse of the Bambino, they will not be content to rest on this feat. They will be motivated to sustain this newly acquired dominant position and start their own dynasty. The Yankees will be determined not to let this happen. The rivalry lives on.

In the early 1920s the Yankees learned that the quest to be number one is made more vivid and tangible by the selection of an enemy organization. Having an adversary motivates the players and hypes fan interest. The Giants played this role as the Yankees established their early dominance and the Boston Red Sox have been a main foe for much of the dynasty, but other organizations (Cleveland Indians and Detroit Tigers on the field, and the Brooklyn Dodgers and New York Mets for fans) have served this purpose as well. In the corporate world, the selection of a top competitor as a visible adversary frequently catalyzes the workforce and drives it to success. Every organization should know its main competition and study this competitor's strategies, tactics, and talent. In baseball, as in business, staying ahead of the competition both on and off the field is the key to sustained success. Making periodic changes in the adversary sustains motivation, keeps the workforce receptive to change, and prevents it from resting on its laurels.

LESSONS FOR YOUR TEAM

How to implement the "Set the Bar Higher Than Your People Have Ever Seen It" principle:

1. Have clear organizational goals that all members of the organization understand and accept. All employees must realize that their individual performance will be measured against their contribution to team goals.

2. Advise each employee as to the behaviors and accomplishments expected of their position. They need to understand how their position contributes to the organization attaining its goals.

3. Make sure your employees understand that organizational triumphs take precedence over individual stardom.

4. Develop critical performance measures for your organization. These go beyond simple statistics and establish contribution to organizational success.

5. Know your competitors' strengths, weaknesses, and accomplishments, and use these measures to motivate your organization. Establish a healthy rivalry with a chief competitor.

6. Establish long-term goals to achieve and maintain organizational success.

CHAPTER

5

Make Organizational Competencies the Heart of Your Appraisal Process: Qualitative Performance Measures

For the Yankees as well as your organization, competencies are the foundation for winning. Competencies are the observable and measurable skills, values, and behaviors that contribute to enhanced employee performance and organizational success. Competencies must be clearly defined, articulated, and embedded throughout your organization.

Earlier chapters discuss how Yankee competencies, as established and exemplified by the principal owner, are key components in the selection of the field manager and team captains. This fifth principle explores how the Yankees use their competencies in the appraisal, selection, and development processes for every member of the organization. These competencies include professional, leadership, and citizenship skills.

Measurement Stems from Organizational Competencies

Waite Hoyt, a Hall of Fame pitcher for the Yankees from 1921 to 1930, stated, "When we were challenged, when we had to win, we stuck together and played with a fury and determination that could only come from team spirit. We had a pride in our performance that was very real. It took on the form of snobbery. We felt we were superior people, and I do believe we left a heritage that became a Yankee tradition." He is referring to the unique Yankee pride that began with the Ruppert ownership and has been the essence of the winning tradition ever since. Hoyt was summarizing the intrinsic values that were instilled in the Yankees by the owner. He understood that the team was not only expected to win but must be capable of winning year after year. His comments encompass not only himself, a superstar contributor, but all his teammates. He went on to state, "The secret to success is to pitch for the New York Yankees." Hoyt realized that Yankee pride had to be part of the equation, for continuous success and values were the foundation of pride.

The fundamental value at the foundation of Yankee pride is winning as a team. Yankee pride also refers to the team's core competencies—the skills, values, and behaviors that are deemed critical to the success of each team member and the success of the entire organization. In the corporate world, these elements are called institutional competencies. They are vital in guiding and sustaining substantial employee contributions to the organization. Like accomplishments, competencies must have dimensions, measures, and standards to ensure that they can be linked to substantial measurable results. They must be explicit, and players must be assessed against these competencies. Management decisions concerning each player must be guided by the assessments. The combination of accomplishment and competency assessment is the basis for player selection, development, career advancement, compensation, and recognition.

Every organization must define its own competencies or success factors in terms of the requirements of its competitive environment. Research by Lance A. Berger & Associates determined that there were probably no more than 30 institutional competencies, with most organizations using between 9 and 11. The most typical corporate competencies are:

- *Action orientation.* Is able to establish and fulfill appropriate tasks to complete projects successfully.

- *Communications.* Is able to convey ideas and concepts clearly and concisely both orally and in written formats.

- *Creativity/innovation.* Generates novel and valuable ideas, and uses the ideas in developing new or improved processes, methods, or systems even when consequences are difficult to measure or predict.

- *Critical judgment.* Defines issues, and focuses on achieving workable solutions.

- *Customer orientation.* Establishes and maintains credibility and trust with customers by producing consistently high-quality products and services designed to meet customer needs.

- *Interpersonal skill.* Develops mutually beneficial relationships with peers, bosses, subordinates, and all others in the work environment. Uses positive communication styles to gain the support of others.

- *Leadership.* Uses appropriate interpersonal styles and methods to inspire and guide others.

- *Teamwork.* Actively participates in teams and other group activities in a positive and constructive way.

- *Technical/job expertise.* Possesses the technical, professional, and business skills, as well as the knowledge, tools, techniques, and theories to function successfully in a specific position.

Yankee competencies evolved over the eight-decade course of the dynasty and overlap with those of the corporate database. They are aligned with the values of the owners, managers, coaches, and captains and fall into three categories: professional, citizenship, and leadership skills (Chapter 1). These are the dimensions. The measures of these dimensions are the competencies, and the minimal standard for all Yankee competencies is "exceeding expectations for the average level of peer player on a competitor team."

Yankee competencies and their dimensions are:

Professional Skills

- Knowledge of and ability to perform the professional skills pertinent to a player's position.

- Commitment to improve skills (practices hard and consistently).

- Acceptance of and willingness to seek coaching to improve skills.

- Basic knowledge of the rules of the game.

Citizenship Skills

- Recognition that the team comes first.

- Commitment to winning.

- Commitment to being a contributing, supportive member of the team.

- Understanding own role in attaining team results.

- Knowledge of and respect for Yankee traditions.

- Respectful treatment of fans and media.

- Understanding that a player's behavior and performance on and off the field affects the customer (fan) team perception.

- Commitment to play hard every day despite personal discomfort.

- Proactively assisting the team in identifying and recruiting high-quality talent.

Leadership Skills

- Poise in difficult situations.

- Willingness to make constructive suggestions to improving the team.

- Respect and support for other players on the team.

- Trust of and trusted by other players.

- Active support of the manager and captain.

- Congenial relationships with other players and management.

Ideally, all Yankee players are measured on these competencies. Their compensation and reputation should be commensurate not only with their accomplishments but also with their competency levels. Historically, the Yankees have had many solid players with average professional skills who exhibited superior strengths in other competencies. These players have had long and illustrious careers on the team. Through their professionalism, citizenship, and leadership, they gained the respect of the manager, teammates, and baseball public. There are too many of these players to note, and though their names have been lost to most casual Yankee fans because they were not superstars or stars, they were and are an essential part of Yankee success.

Managers Miller Huggins, Joe McCarthy, and Casey Stengel all demanded strict adherence to the Yankee Way. They did not tolerate player behaviors that would destabilize the team. They were willing to take the necessary actions to ensure that players fully understood and conformed to expectations.

Miller Huggins' Personal Code Is the Foundation for the Yankee Way

Huggins built the foundation for Yankee greatness. He set forth a code for all managers to follow and was a role model for Yankee competencies. The main behaviors that Huggins promulgated were based on his experiences as a player:

- Always strive to win.
- Put the team first.
- Stay poised in difficult situations.
- Respect, trust, and support your teammates.
- Maintain cordial relationships with teammates and management.
- Commit to improving professional skills.

Huggins' code came from his work ethic as a player. That he overcame his diminutive stature to succeed in a game of superior athletes was reaffirmed in his managerial skills. Huggins excelled by outwitting the opponents, by maximizing the advantages he did have, and by sheer force of will. As a player, one example of his determination was the process by which he became a switch hitter. He was right-handed but decided to learn to hit left-handed so he would be a step closer to first base. He went through a grueling training routine to teach his muscles to respond to left-handed domination. Huggins was committed to winning, understood how he could best use his abilities to help his team win, and was determined to do everything within his power to be the best player he could be. He made his size an advantage by patiently working pitchers for walks to get on base. As a manager, he outwitted his opponents by coaching his players to adapt their hitting and fielding to the opposition's strengths and weaknesses. Huggins understood how winning teams play baseball.

Huggins was a strict disciplinarian who lived what he preached. He had remarkable insight into human behavior and psychology, as evidenced by his leadership skills. He established behavioral expectations for all his players and enforced these rules equally and fairly. Huggins believed that if any one player had different rules, the manager would never be able to establish his own authority. His equitable treatment gained him the trust and respect of his team, management, and fans.

Joe McCarthy's Ten Rules for Baseball Success

Joe McCarthy recognized the competencies that led to Yankee greatness and enforced "behavior befitting a Yankee" unequivocally. McCarthy understood that player behavior was inextricably linked to clear expectations for success. McCarthy knew that his tactical and strategic managerial skills would be useless unless he concretely connected his expectations to player behavior. He formulated a set of practical rules that players could follow to sustain success. The rules were called "Joe McCarthy's Ten Commandments for Success in

Baseball." They are McCarthy's interpretation of the professional, leadership, and citizenship competencies at the core of Yankee success. McCarthy's 10 rules are posted in the Baseball Hall of Fame and are listed here along with translations of the behaviors that are pertinent to the business world.

1. Nobody ever became a ballplayer by walking after a ball. *Translation: Always be engaged in the action and give your best to succeed.*

2. You will never become a .300 hitter unless you take the bat off your shoulder. *Translation: If you don't try, you can't possibly succeed.*

3. An outfielder who throws in back of a runner is locking the barn after the horse is stolen. *Translation: Be proactive. Take action when opportunities are presented.*

4. Keep your head up and you may not have to keep it down. *Translation: Stay alert for opportunities and obstacles.*

5. When you start to slide, slide. He who changes his mind may have to change a good leg for a bad one. *Translation: Be decisive, follow through, and finish what you start.*

6. Do not alibi on bad hops. Anybody can field the good ones. *Translation: Accept your failures, especially in difficult situations; be modest with success.*

7. Always run them out. You never can tell. *Translation: Follow through on assignments even when a successful conclusion seems hazy. Expect to succeed even when success seems impossible.*

8. Do not quit. *No translation needed.*

9. Do not fight too much with the umpires. You cannot expect them to be as perfect as you are. *Translation: Don't waste your*

energy on things that cannot be changed or controlled. Accept the decisions of those with authority and move on; decisions are made by human beings.

10. A pitcher who hasn't control hasn't anything. *Translation: Work at improving your professional skills; use discipline and focus on achieving your professional goals.*

Casey Stengel: A Clownish Approach to Imparting Competencies

It would seem incongruous that Casey Stengel with his comedic approach would be the purveyor of the Yankee Way, but he succeeded in passing on Yankee competencies in his offbeat style. His clownish demeanor was his unique device for imparting the Yankee Way. He believed the most effective way to carry on the Yankee Way was through a mentoring approach that used veteran players, stars, and superstars to develop the Yankee competencies in other players. The most visible symbol of this was the instructional school for rookies that he initiated in 1949 to give new players individualized competency training. Stengel also emphasized a team orientation by forcing players to adapt to his unique approach of alternating players based on the competitive situation. He recognized the strengths and weaknesses of his players and used them accordingly. Stengel liked to rotate four or five outfielders. If one went into a batting slump, someone else immediately filled his slot. Team citizenship was high on Stengel's competency list. Stengel realized that developing citizenship skills didn't always equate with manager popularity. Stengel stated, "The secret of managing is to keep the guys who hate you away from the guys who are undecided."

Joe Torre's Teams Are Shaped around Core Competencies

Recent Yankee teams are modeled very closely around the described core competencies and traditional values that serve as the team's heritage and backbone. Joe Torre believes that a team approach is the key to managerial success in developing player competencies, stating, "The manager must put loyalty to the team above loyalty to any one player."

Under Torre each player is imbued with the Yankee core competencies and values. As he pointed out when comparing his teams with past dynasty teams, "Just having marquee players is not enough. You need to have a team that can play as a unit." Superstars, stars, and solid players equally respect and adhere to the disciplined, supportive principles that enable the team to function as a winning, well-oiled machine. Superstar Derek Jeter stated it best when he said, "The Yankees have 25 heroes." Players work hard on and off the field to maintain the Yankee traditional image.

Teams like the 2000 Yankees are a stellar example of what Yankee winning based on a perpetuation of Yankee values and competencies is all about. They won the World Series with some outstanding players at key positions like pitchers Roger Clemens, David Cone, and Andy Pettitte, catcher Jorge Posada, and superstar shortstop Derek Jeter, yet most of the players were not at this level. Torre said, "We may not have the best players, but we certainly have the best team." George Steinbrenner, owner and man of few compliments, stated, "These guys had a team concept that was tremendous. I've had better teams, but none with a bigger heart."

Dysfunctional Behaviors Can Hurt the Team

The Yankees also have had their share of superstar players who have exhibited extraordinary accomplishments but were lacking in Yankee competencies. Babe Ruth is one such player. Ruth is perhaps the greatest baseball player in the history of the game. He is legendary for signing autographs, mingling with fans, and even pointing to areas in the bleachers to target his mighty home runs. However, when it came to coachability, taking direction, teamwork, and especially integrity, Ruth also is legendary but in a much less favorable light. He had a reputation for overeating, overindulging in alcohol consumption, and indiscriminate womanizing. He also was insubordinate to all levels of the Yankee hierarchy. Ruth, frustrated by a batting slump, once went into the stands after a heckling fan. He had dugout brawls with his teammates, and lacked restraint when he did not agree with umpires' calls. In 1922 his behavior was so reckless that he was suspended five times. Ruth had a most disruptive and destabilizing effect on the team but was tolerated because of his epic hitting contribution and his fan attraction. It is unlikely that any other player would have remained a Yankee with such poor citizenship and leadership competencies.

Nobody questions Ruth's enormous contribution to attaining and winning championships, but even this legend did not optimize his potential and achieve all his goals because of his unwillingness or inability to develop or adapt his behaviors to conform to Yankee values. Ruth wanted to be a Yankee manager and was constantly thwarted in this pursuit by Yankee ownership that recognized his shortcomings and would not jeopardize the team reputation or success by appointing him to the position.

The team was constantly destabilized by Ruth's disruptive behaviors and its influence on his teammates. He feuded with Joe

McCarthy, the Yankee manager, and even with Lou Gehrig, once his close friend and admirer. The owners cut Ruth's enormous salary considerably for two successive years and ultimately traded Ruth to the Boston Braves. Once this superstar lost his hitting prowess, his lack of other competencies made him a liability. Ruth, who at one time hoped to be a Yankee manager, failed to grasp the basic citizenship and leadership requirements the position required.

Another flawed Yankee superstar was Reggie Jackson. The baseball community knows Jackson as "Mr. October" because of his heroics (clutch hitting) in winning World Series. He had his best performances when the stakes were highest and the audience was largest. He hit three home runs on three pitches in the final game of the 1977 World Series to beat the Dodgers. However, Jackson was an outspoken egomaniac. He was insubordinate to and fought with his owners and his managers, especially Billy Martin. The whole team resented Jackson's egotistical boasting. The outfielder exclaimed in a magazine article that he was "the straw that stirs the drink" and ridiculed his teammates in the same article for aspiring to replace Jackson in this role. Jackson always considered himself above the good of his team. He would sulk and react with unsportsmanlike conduct when his manager moved him from the cleanup position in the lineup or took him off the field as a designated hitter. He was not behaving like a Yankee.

The Yankee clubhouse would have been a much more serene environment if Ruth and Jackson had exhibited other Yankee competencies beyond outstanding accomplishments. Many sports experts believe that had Ruth and Jackson possessed the full complement of Yankee competencies, their teams would have been even more successful.

In 2004 the Yankees acquired star pitcher Kevin Brown. In a fit of self-directed anger over a poor game performance, Brown punched a concrete wall and broke his nonpitching hand. Although he apologized to the team, ownership, and fans for his selfish behavior, his performance for the balance of the season was marginalized and may have cost the team an appearance in yet another World Series. His reprimand, if any, was not made public. Brown's behavior was distinctly not Yankee-like. The Yankees should have known better than to trade for Brown because his troublesome reputation preceded him. His behavior was disappointing but it was not unexpected by anyone familiar with his history. Brown is an example of a star lacking adequate citizenship and leadership competencies. Management did not follow their own principles of success when they selected him. More than one Kevin Brown type of player could put any team into a downward spiral.

Measure Your Employees Based on Organizational Competencies and Values

Every team or company has its core values and competencies that set it apart from its competitors. Organizations need to identify and develop these competencies and values. They need to share these required behaviors with every level of the organization. Every player or worker must know that his or her performance is measured against these behaviors and his or her reward package is commensurate with exhibited behaviors. Organizations cannot overlook insubordinate behavior or poor relationship skills even from a supersalesperson or a world-class scientist, because their negative influence could threaten morale and become a detriment to long-term success. The Yankees attempted discipline and coaching to minimize citizenship and leadership problems but were marginally successful. Aberrant superstars and stars in more traditional organizations not required to be part of ongoing social interactions are typically isolated and encouraged to focus on non-people-related tasks. Others that do require social interaction rarely last for long periods of time. Reggie Jackson wore out his stay in five tumultuous years.

Validating Your Competencies

The Yankee teams did not go through a rigorous statistical validation process to confirm the linkage of their competencies to hard measures of success. They trusted in the cumulative observations of astute members of their winning organizations to surface the essential qualities that contributed to the successful performance of their obvious role models. They proceeded to convert these observations into a clear set of expectations for all Yankee players. This is a process that can be used by managers in any organization.

LESSONS FOR YOUR TEAM

How to implement the "Make Organizational Competencies the Heart of Your Appraisal Process" principle:

1. Define your competencies or success factors in terms of the requirements of the competitive environment. These core competencies are expectations of behaviors, skills, or values that are crucial to the success of your entire organization.

2. Establish expected behaviors for each core competency and then determine the level of competency proficiency for each position in the organization.

3. Use these competencies to select new employees and to evaluate existing employees in terms of their current or future contributions to the organization.

4. Develop, compensate, promote, and recognize employees based on a combination of actual performance and competency assessment.

5. Ensure that employees understand organizational competencies. This understanding is part of being a company's good citizen.

6. Provide periodic feedback to employees on their measurement against core competencies.

7. Establish organization-wide training, development, coaching, and mentoring programs to close employee competency gaps.

8. Evaluate the benefits and costs of keeping employees with outstanding accomplishments but major inadequacies in other competency areas. Consider the long-term cost/benefit effects of such individuals.

CHAPTER

6

Make Everyone on the Team a Talent Scout

One of the major sources of differentiation possessed by the Yankees is their ability to scout and assess talent. This chapter focuses on how the Yankees are able to consistently maintain a high-quality team through their own special approach. We look at their scouting methods and the importance of employing talented talent scouts. We also examine the Yankee secret strategy: Everyone on the team is a talent scout.

Your organization can expand its scouting field beyond the formal conduits by instilling talent assessment and scouting as an organizational value. Employees must understand their potential critical role in bringing fresh talent into your company.

In the Yankee organization, scouting, appraising, selecting, and placing talent occurs in two ways. The Yankees, like most teams, have a formal global network of scouts whose purpose is to find potential major league players who meet the expectations of the team. Professional scouts have their distinct function in the Yankee organization, but their role is augmented by the input of other Yankee personnel. That's the second way that the Yankees approach talent management. In the Yankee organization, everyone is constantly identifying, recommending, and even actively recruiting talent both within and outside the organization. The players, the owners, the manager, and the coaches are all constantly on the lookout for ways to improve the team. The result is a vast network of referrals and assessments that ultimately lead to a better ball club. Let's first look at the traditional formal network of scouts.

Professional Scouting: Guarding the Entrance to the Palace

The Yankees must deal with a team that is constantly in flux because of injuries, age, competitor pirating, and payroll costs. As a result, they are constantly focused on maintaining a reservoir of qualified talent. It is not surprising, therefore, that the size of the Yankee formal professional scouting staff represents a disproportionate percentage of the overall organization when compared to a traditional corporation. Some of the Yankee scouts are full-time employees, others are part-time, and still others are contract employees.

As with most things involving the dynasty, the tradition of solid scouting was set more than 70 years ago. George Weiss was hired by Ed Barrow in 1932 to be the general manager of the club's minor league teams. Weiss already had a reputation for being a genius at developing and retaining superior players while selling off surplus talent. As a minor league executive he was particularly adept at realizing where his teams had surplus talent, and then selling that surplus talent to other teams while maintaining his team's level of success. In a 13-year minor league span Weiss had sold players for more than half a million dollars while his teams stayed competitive. Dozens of prospects discovered by Weiss developed into major league players.

Weiss then brought his talents to the Yankees and served as general manager from 1947 to 1960. At the zenith of Weiss' minor league organization, the Yankees had 20 teams feeding talent to the parent club. From this stream, Weiss would sell or trade surplus players or players who did not fit into the Yankee long- or short-term plans. Weiss' skill at selecting, developing, and retaining players and establishing parameters for the scouting system would have a lasting impact on the Yankee dynasty.

Professional Scouts Discover Diamonds in the Rough

Scouts are measured by the quality of their referrals, and by that measure Tom Greenwade was one of the greatest of baseball's scouts. Greenwade was the epitome of the scouting professional. He possessed an intuitive ability to assess qualifications. He had a wide, varied network of acquaintances that included high school coaches, minor league managers, and umpires who referred potential talent to him. He understood and completely bought into the Yankee success model and he searched for players who matched the model. His task was to delve into the uncertain world of assessing players' potential based on limited amounts of data. He followed up on all leads and was willing to give a young player a second look. Furthermore, he moved in to sign his prospects before other scouts could contact them and start competitive bidding. He discovered and signed Mickey Mantle, Elston Howard, and many others in the 1940s and 1950s. His perseverance and intuition in scouting and signing top prospects allowed the dynasty to continue unabated in the post–World War II era.

The Yankee scouting skills also enabled the organization to sign for minimal salaries many prospects overlooked by or invisible to other organizations. Greenwade had ongoing contact with many managers in the country's bush leagues. He first heard of Mickey Mantle when Mantle was only 16 years old and still in high school. He immediately went to watch him pitch and play shortstop. Greenwade was unimpressed at first viewing but kept Mantle on his radar screen. He was reminded the following year by one of his contacts, an umpire who had seen Mantle play, that he should be sure to observe Mantle again. Mantle had now matured and was starting to blossom as a player. Greenwade inquired when Mantle would be graduating from high school and showed up at his parents' home the morning of graduation. He was relieved to hear no other scouts had been to call. He went with the Mantle family to a game in which Mantle was playing immediately after graduation.

Greenwade looked into his crystal ball and saw in Mantle's raw talent a superstar in the making. He was a player with unmatched speed and power and he also possessed competencies that would make him eager to follow the Yankee Way. Greenwade signed Mantle to a contract to play in the Kansas Class D Yankee farm system.

Another highly successful and perceptive Yankee scout was Paul Krichell, the man responsible for signing Lou Gehrig. Gehrig was a star pitcher for Columbia University. Krichell was one of a few spectators present at one of Gehrig's college games when he struck out 17 batters. College players were rarely scouted during Krichell's era, so he was ahead of his time in tapping into this source of talent. What especially impressed Krichell, however, was Gehrig's batting prowess. In a manner reminiscent of Barrow's projection of Babe Ruth from a pitcher to an outfielder, Krichell made a similar verdict on Gehrig. Within days of this game, Krichell signed Gehrig to a Yankee contract.

One of Krichell's biggest bargains and crucial signings was Phil Rizzuto. Rizzuto was a diminutive shortstop who described himself as "not very big for a little guy." Because of his small physical stature most scouts undervalued Rizzuto's potential. Yet he was the master of some very critical skills that the team needed. He was an ace at the bunt and hit-and-run in an era when the power hitter was king.

Krichell first noticed Rizzuto when he was a star for his Brooklyn high school baseball team. Krichell saw the tenacity of Miller Huggins in Rizzuto. In 1937, Rizzuto's high school coach begged New York's three teams to give Rizzuto a tryout. Both the Dodgers and the Giants dismissed him. Based on Krichell's previous assessment, the Yankees offered Rizzuto a tryout. Rizzuto's performance at the tryout was enough to impress Krichell. He signed Rizzuto for what Ed Barrow said was "20 cents, the cost of his lunch at the tryout." Krichell's "smell for talent," his understanding of Yankee special competencies, and his willingness to take a risk on talent passed over by others made him a scouting genius. Rizzuto proved Krichell correct. Krichell also signed Tony Lazzeri and Whitey Ford in addition to Gehrig and Rizzuto—four Hall of Fame players from one scout.

The Yankees assess their scouts based on the accomplishments of the players they recommend. In traditional organizations the internal and external recruiters, and managers, should also be measured against the quality of the employees they recommend for hire. Their "batting average" for finding corporate superstars, stars, and solid players is their scorecard. Corporations need to find, position, and recognize people like Tom Greenwade and Paul Krichell in their organizations. Having people who possess a large network of re-cruiters and acquaintances who can refer talent is an invaluable asset. When a prospect develops into a superstar, recruiters and managers should be rewarded both financially and with organization-wide recognition for their efforts.

The Yankee Scouting System

The Yankees, through a series of hierarchical feeder organizations called farm teams, are able to integrate external talent from many dif-ferent areas. These minor league teams have labels like A, AA, and AAA. They are the rough equivalent of entry, middle, and upper management levels in a traditional organization. The parent baseball team corresponds to executive management. The farm teams' primary purpose is to generate a flow of qualified players to the next level in a cost-effective way.

The Yankees, like all teams, send out their scouts to watch thou-sands of high school and college baseball games every season. They at-tend amateur baseball games and the Little League World Series. Often, promising players are invited to a tryout where their skills are further assessed with no obligation from the team. Sometimes, as in the case of Mickey Mantle, players are signed right out of high school, but more typically, as in the case of Lou Gehrig, they are plucked out of college.

An internship program at a company is like a minor league stint in baseball. Top candidates in their high school or college classes are hired by companies for entry-level jobs usually for no or very small wages to assess their potential for joining the corporate team. The candidate has an opportunity to make an impression on the organiza-tion while gaining invaluable experience. Companies have no obligation to hire the intern beyond the contracted period, but are able to determine firsthand if the intern has the potential to be a productive member of the organization.

The Yankees Go Global

The quest for superstars and stars led the Yankees to extend their scouting to other countries. They have become a model for any organization seeking to identify superstars and stars beyond its immediate borders. The first purveyor of the wide scouting net was George Steinbrenner. Under Steinbrenner, the Yankees became skillful in both assessing and recruiting foreign-born talent.

The richest source of talent has been Latin America. This region has boasted an interest in baseball since the 1870s. Cubans, for example, have been playing baseball since before the Spanish-American War. The 2004 Yankees boast high-quality players like Mariano Rivera (Panama), Bernie Williams and Jorge Posada (Puerto Rico), Miguel Cairo (Venezuela), Felix Heredia and Enrique Wilson (Dominican Republic), and Orlando "El Duque" Hernandez (Cuba), among the players who have come from this region. The Yankees are also aware that major league players have been recruited from Colombia, Mexico, Virgin Islands, Nicaragua, Honduras, Curaçao, Belize, and Aruba. They include these areas in their zone of scouting. The next Yankee superstar may come from one of these regions.

Several countries in Latin America have winter baseball leagues. These leagues provide good opportunities for the Yankees to scout local and regional talent. In the corporate world the analogue of the winter leagues would be regional management and technical conferences that host groups of high-quality people.

While Latin America is a principal focus of Yankee scouts, it is not the only non-U.S. region. Canada, Japan, Korea, Australia, and Taiwan are also on the team's radar screen. All of these countries have extensive amateur baseball leagues similar to their counterparts in the United States.

The Toronto Blue Jays is a Major League Baseball franchise, and the Montreal Expos played in the major league from 1969 until the close of the 2004 season. Canada also has a well-organized and extensive collection of amateur leagues under the umbrella of the Canadian Federation of Amateur Baseball. Babe Ruth's replacement in 1934 was Canadian George Selkirk.

Japan's talent has recently come under the intense focus of the Yankees' scouting microscope. The Yankees played two regular-season games in Japan in 2004. It was a great opportunity to merchandise the team to baseball fans and potential players. Baseball has been played in Japan since the 1870s and has flourished since that time. The Yankees' first and somewhat unsuccessful Japanese recruit was pitcher Hideki Irabu. Although Irabu was a member of the 1998 and 1999 World Champion Yankees, his performance never met expectations. Yankee management understood the marketing possibilities from having a Japanese player and endorsed his signing despite assessments that indicated weak citizenship and leadership competencies reflected in deficiencies in work ethic and winning attitude. The second and highly successful Japanese recruit, Hideki Matsui, is a model of the Yankee Way. His performance clearly meets expectations, and many fans point out that his stoic demeanor and quiet leadership are reminiscent of Lou Gehrig. Despite obvious cultural differences, Matsui's manner makes him a perfect fit for a Yankee team captained by Derek Jeter.

The Yankees' scouting experience clearly advances the notion that a winning organization with a strong set of competencies, a sophisticated staffing system, and an open mind can find, recruit, develop, and acculturate players from diverse sources of recruitment.

Scouting: A Managerial Competency

Field managers in particular are held responsible for selecting and developing future team stars. All managers throughout the Yankee major and minor league system have talent assessment as part of their job descriptions. Their movement to higher managerial levels is heavily dependent on their ability to scout talent. Their judgments contribute to the organizational goal of constantly backing up positions at all levels of the organization with the most competent people. Furthermore, the managers take ownership for their talent discoveries and make it their job to develop these prospects. The ability to recognize talent has been a cardinal strength of successful Yankee managers.

Miller Huggins

Miller Huggins had an intuitive ability to spot and evaluate talent. He rarely traded away players who became stars elsewhere. Two rare exceptions were pitcher Urban Shocker, who won 20 or more games four years in a row for the St. Louis Browns, and catcher Muddy Ruel, who starred on the Washington Senators' pennant-winning team in 1924 and 1925. Miller acknowledged his mistake in both cases and attempted to reacquire Shocker, which he did after the 1924 season. He also traded for players who turned out to be far more talented than was generally expected. The talented pitchers who were acquired from the Red Sox, and were crucial for the Yankee division titles in the 1920s, were considered equitable trades at the time—even in the Boston press.

When Huggins spotted potential talent, he stuck with that man for a long time. George Pipgras was one of those players. Pipgras was a pitcher acquired from the Red Sox in 1923. In the next four years, he won only one game for the Yankees, spending much time in the minor leagues working on his control. He won 10 games for the 1927 Yankees and in 1928 led the league with 24 wins.

In the mid-1920s, when teams were afraid or unwilling to trade with the Yankees, Huggins was adept at identifying talent from the minor leagues. His later pennant-winning teams in 1926, 1927, and 1928 were built around Lou Gehrig, Tony Lazzeri, and Earle Combs. They all joined the Yankees before playing a major league game with another team and all became Hall of Fame honorees.

Casey Stengel

In 1950, the Yankees under Casey Stengel opened an early spring camp in Phoenix before spring training began in Florida. Stengel called the camp an instructional school and used it as an opportunity to train new recruits in the Yankee Way and scout out potential replacements for his roster players. As defending World Champions, the executive suite felt the Yankees didn't need much help, but Stengel was determined to have young players waiting in the wings, ready for the day when the pitching staff would grow old and when the veterans like Joe DiMaggio would retire.

Stengel had received a letter from a young player named Ed Ford. In his letter, Ford stated his ability to help the Yankees win the pennant. Stengel invited Ford to the instructional school in Phoenix to prove his worth to the team, and was impressed by Ford's confidence and pitching skills. Stengel was instrumental in having Ford signed. Ed "Whitey" Ford became a Hall of Famer after a 16-year career pitching for the Yankees.

Stengel's strength as a manager was not only the ability to recognize potential greatness but his desire to optimize the solid players as well as the stars. Stengel, explaining his managerial philosophy, stated, "The first 15 guys on a club you don't have to bother with. They're always playing and don't need the manager. The next five play once in a while, so you gotta spend some time buttering them up. The last five you gotta be with all the time."

Everyone Is a Scout

In the Yankee organization, not just the managers identify, recruit, and select talent. Everyone on the team realizes the necessity of keeping a steady flow of talent to the major league club. Individual players are always contacting players on other teams whom the Yankees are trying to trade for or sign. When the Yankees were pursuing Alex Rodriguez before the 2004 season, several players called Rodriguez to let him know that the Yankees were a winning organization and one where he would feel at home. Even after A-Rod's signing, players continued to take personal responsibility for introducing him to the Yankee Way.

In traditional organizations, the conduit for scouting external talent is typically recruiters and headhunters. However, organizations should formalize their scouting process under the human resources department, and all employees should be aware of their role in it. Scouting should be part of every employee's citizenship competency.

Informally, employees and managers make referrals based on their personal network of professional contacts, friends, and relatives. The process is typically unorganized and at best rudimentary. There is usually no formal process for managers and employees to take note of people whom they encounter at professional meetings, conferences, and social events who could meet the institutional competencies of the organization. Such a list could amplify the internal candidate list. This could become especially useful in the case of qualified employees who are members of diverse groups. In addition, the company should sponsor their employees' attendance at events and meetings where employees might come into contact with potential recruits. All employees must be versed in the competencies and values of the organization and be able to recognize them in others.

Another way an organization can add to the talent pool is to collect and store all resumes submitted for job openings, responding with company literature and a thank-you note to all applicants. This provides applicants with a positive view of the organization, and the organization with a pool of future candidates and a reservoir of goodwill that extends beyond the original applicant. The resume may not fit with current job openings, but may mesh with an opening at another time.

LESSONS FOR YOUR TEAM

How to implement the "Make Everyone on the Team a Talent Scout" principle:

1. Ensure that every employee knows that talent assessment and scouting are organizational values.

2. Value talent assessment as a key role of every employee through special recognition and rewards.

3. Send employees to industry meetings and conventions where they have an opportunity to serve as company ambassadors, identify potential employees, and establish valuable networks for recruiting.

4. Establish internship programs to identify high school and college talent.

5. Consider extending your scouting horizons. The Internet can expand your recruiting contacts.

6. Establish a formal process for collecting and utilizing scouting information from as many sources as possible.

CHAPTER 7

Create a Balance of Superstars, Stars, and Solid Performers: Assessing and Classifying Your Employees

You hear it all the time: "The Yankees are a team of all-stars." "The Yankees just buy other teams' superstars." "They have a superstar at every position." However, despite what many detractors believe to be the key to the Yankee dynasty, there are not enough superstars in the baseball player pool for the Yankees to buy and field a team of only superstars. The Yankee dynasty teams have been developed around a blend of players at varying performance levels: superstars, stars, and solid performers. Granted, the Yankees know the value of having a few superstars on the team, but far more important to Yankee success is how they use various types of players to win baseball games. This chapter looks at how the Yankees continually classify and reclassify players and use these categorizations to create a dynastic team with the right blend of talent. Every organization, including the Yankees (despite its reputation to the contrary), has finite dollars to be spent on its workforce, so it must use its money wisely.

The mechanics of converting the player classifications developed in this chapter into a talent plan is presented in Chapter 8 and the conversion of the talent plan into a compensation program is outlined in Chapter 10.

The Yankee mystique suggests that it has been a team of superstars (Hall of Fame level players) but the facts do not support this perception. It is impossible for the Yankees or any team to accomplish this feat because, by definition, the pool of superstars is always limited (probably no more than 2 percent to 4 percent of Major League Baseball players at any given time), not all positions have available superstars, and not all superstars can or would play for the Yankees. The reality is that Yankee success has resulted from skillful development and management of teams that reflect a careful blend of a very small number of superstars, several stars, and many solid players. Highly entrepreneurial ownership and adept management have been able to carefully find, using the Yankees' own de facto competency profile (accomplishments, professional skills, citizenship, and leadership), the required players to successfully fill all positions. The whole Yankee team performs better than the sum of its parts.

The Yankee team construction begins with scouting and assessing its own and competitor talent against its targeted competencies. In this principle, the classification of actual and potential contributions of every player to the organization is the first step in constructing the team composition. The classification of talent is necessary before the organization can shape its people strategy.

Accomplishments and Professional Skills

When referring to players as superstars, stars, or solid players, most fans consider fielding, pitching, or batting accomplishments. In baseball, accomplishments are typically defined in statistical comparisons. Major statistical accomplishments are measurable and visible to the media and the fans. Everyone is privy to and understands a batter's home run output, his batting average, or the number of runs he has batted in. How many times a hitter delivers in the clutch (a high-quality hit) and the player's on-base percentage are more subtle measures of a batter's contribution to his team. A pitcher's won-lost record, his strikeouts, and his walks are statistics the media and fans point out when evaluating the pitcher's merit. However, for pitchers, statistics such as the quality of the opponents in a pitcher's win are considered by the franchise when evaluating his value to the team. Baseball management must delve below the basic published statistics to determine a player's true worth to his team. As in baseball, all managers should attempt to assess less obvious accomplishments as well as more explicit achievements in order to determine accurate employee value.

In addition to measurable accomplishments, teams assess players on the basis of their professional skills. This is necessary because of the high correlation between professional skills and accomplishments. By improving player professional skills the team should see a concomitant improvement in accomplishments. However, a batter can have a perfect swing and appear professionally competent but his batting average and home run output may be low. A pitcher may have an incredible fastball but rarely throw strikes or get batters out. The lack of production in the presence of sound professional skills could be the result of issues involving citizenship, leadership, physical, or personal problems. Organizations must consider current and projected accomplishments (performance) and professional proficiencies when classifying its talent pool in terms of superstars, stars, and solid players.

When professional skills erode or become obsolete, the player will not sustain his level of team contribution. The team must adjust its mix of talent to allow for a downgraded player to continue on the team or consider trading or dropping the player. The task of managing the talent mix becomes increasingly difficult when a player does not accept the reality of diminished skills and expects a continued level of previous recognition in the form of salary and innings played. This sometimes manifests itself in ignoring citizenship and leadership expectations, resulting in team distraction and a departure from the winning tradition. Other problems emerging from eroding skills can be a player's unwillingness to work and practice hard, accept coaching, and adjust playing time. These factors, too, can cause performance problems and loss of credibility with teammates, management, and fans.

When a franchise can optimize the performance of fading superstars and stars through changing the team mix, it can maintain high levels of performance. The Yankee dynasty has been boosted by management proficiency at adding aging superstars and stars to emerging and current superstars and stars. For example, the Yankees in the early 1950s used the aging Johnny Mize, once superstar and future Hall of Fame inductee, as a part-time star and in the 1990s used the aging Wade Boggs, also a future Hall of Fame honoree, as a full-time star. The Yankees have successfully utilized aging players numerous times in their dynasty years. The Yankee management is also adept at divesting solid players whose accomplishments and skills erode below the competitive levels required to remain on the team before they can diminish the team's performance.

Superstars

Players whose accomplishments and professional skills greatly exceed those of the best past and present players are superstars. They will be enshrined in the Baseball Hall of Fame and their reputations extend beyond their own fan base. They should be at least solid citizens and leader supportive. They have very high attraction and retention value. A special type of superstar can be labeled a *super-stalwart*. Super-stalwarts demonstrate much more than a high level of accomplishment and professional excellence. They inspire others to superior performance (leadership) and are role models for the organization's values (citizenship). Based on this definition, superstars Babe Ruth, Joe DiMaggio, Mickey Mantle, and Reggie Jackson would not be super-stalwarts because their strengths in leadership and citizenship were not at the same high level as their accomplishments and professional skills. They were high-level performers with high-end retention value, but their overall value diminished precipitously as their professional skills eroded. Lou Gehrig and Derek Jeter are the best examples of super-stalwarts and, not uncoincidentally, were appointed as team captains. Likewise Ruth, DiMaggio, Mantle, and Jackson never assumed a management or leadership position in baseball, or anywhere else, after they retired. Mantle and Jackson were used in promoting the Yankee history of excellence with younger players and the public when their playing days were over but were utilized to coach professional skills and transmit folklore rather than serving as citizenship role models.

The loss or absence of a superstar, or worse a super-stalwart, for any period of time has a disproportionate impact on the team because it disrupts performance directly and no other player is able to replace the super-person's contribution. Other players on the team sometimes lose confidence in the team's ability to win without the superstar; this is most likely an accurate belief. A team with a dynastic vision should continually have at least one superstar and, even better, a super-stalwart. Generally, at any given time the Yankees had between two and four superstars during their dynastic years. They rarely had super-stalwarts and when present these very rare talents were the real drivers of the dynasty and carried the title of captain. Without a captain the managers assumed the burden of leadership but generally had active support of players with better than average leadership skills and a group of largely cooperative solid citizens. The former group of players

had substantial positive influence with other players but their leadership skills did not reach stalwart level.

When a superstar's skills start to erode, he can still be valuable at
the star level for the team as long as his citizenship and leadership
skills remain intact and he accepts a change in classification for the
benefit of the team. A good example of such a player is Wade Boggs.
He moved from superstar to star level and continued to perform as a
major Yankee contributor. He had high expectations for his teammates' performances and an exemplary work ethic. As a Yankee, he
contributed to a World Championship and three postseason series in
his five-year tenure. Boggs' only World Series was with the Yankees.

The Yankee dynastic success suggests that a winning team
should have superstars in at least 4 percent of its roster. A single
super-stalwart will increase the probability that the dynasty will be
sustained.

Stars

Players whose accomplishments and professional skills clearly exceed
those of most current players in competitor organizations are stars.
They, too, must meet the citizenship and leadership requirements of
the team. When stars can lead other people to better accomplishment
and more than adequately represent the values of the team they are
called *star-stalwarts*. Near Hall of Fame players like Thurman Munson
and Don Mattingly were star-stalwarts. They were anointed as captains because of their intense desire to win, strong work ethic, and
desire to continuously improve their own and their teammates' performances. Unfortunately for Mattingly, his Yankee tenure occurred
during the second Yankee dark age. His leadership and winning spirit
infused his teammates with hope and a "never say die" determination.

The 80-plus-year Yankee history suggests that at least 10 percent of the team roster should be stars.

Solid Players

Players who have accomplishments that at least equal those of the average players on other teams, who get along reasonably well with team members and management, and who embrace the team's citizenship expectations are solid players. A large percentage of the Yankee players during the 80-plus-year dynasty fit this category. Only the most ardent Yankee fans and their detractors know the names and accomplishments of solid players once their playing days are over, but their contributions are an integral part of the Yankee dynasty. An example of solid player contribution was made by Bucky Dent, Yankee shortstop from 1977 to 1982. In 1978 Dent hit a crucial home run to help the Yankees win a critical season-ending game to enable them to move on to play in the World Series. He also contributed significantly to winning the World Series and was its Most Valuable Player. There are numerous Bucky Dents in Yankee history, players who had short-term outstanding accomplishments in crucial situations. Dent's accomplishments in clutch situations illustrate the potential for accomplishment of solid players in any organization. During the Yankee dynasty, about 85 percent of the entire team (including the reserves on the bench) would be classified as solid players.

Oddballs

Team members who are below the level of players on competitor teams for accomplishments, professional skills, citizenship values, and/or leadership competencies are considered oddballs. These players can be troublesome and can distract from a winning team effort. The easiest solution to poor performance is termination or trade. The possible answer to weakening professional skills, diminished accomplishments, questionable citizenship values, and deficient leadership is practice, training, development, coaching, and mentoring. Only if these actions bring the player up to solid player standards should the player be retained.

Organizations struggle with some oddballs because their overall level of accomplishment and professional skills is great but poor citizenship and leadership behaviors destabilize the team. When superstars and stars are disruptive influences, they can be referred to as *star-warts*; they leave a negative mark on the team. Sometimes direct feedback, coaching, and mentoring will help the star-wart, but in most cases the best move for long-term team success is trade or termination.

Babe Ruth and Reggie Jackson are examples of oddball superstar-warts that the Yankee management tolerated because of their accomplishments and ability to generate fan and media attention. The Yankees also attempted to reform these players, but with minimal success. Their behavior directly led to management upheaval and teammate discontent. Jackson lasted for five years and Ruth lasted for 15 years with the Yankees.

Jackson provided accomplishments that led to short-term team success, but his egotistical behavior was a source of distraction and low morale. Gabe Paul, the man most responsible for leading the Yankees out of a low period from the early 1960s to the mid-1970s, stepped down as Yankee president in response to the constant state of crisis caused by Jackson, Billy Martin, and George Steinbrenner.

Ruth is a special case because he was a transformational superstar. His monumental accomplishments and fan-friendly personality helped save baseball after a major scandal, and he changed the game from a singles orientation to home run domination. Ruth is a legendary ballplayer. Few if any superstars would receive Ruth's level of management toleration given his lack of self-discipline, extraordinary demands, poor influence on his teammates, and insubordination to management, coaches, and peers.

Player Classification

The Yankees have historically been successful at selecting and developing players against a broader array of characteristics than simply current or projected accomplishments and professional skills. Their approach has been similar to that used at modern corporations with sophisticated talent management systems. The players are classified in terms of their actual and potential contribution. The approach incorporates citizenship and leadership skills in the assessment process. Combining professional skills and accomplishments with other competencies represents a player's attraction and retention value. The use of attraction and retention values as part of a player classification system makes for a higher-quality assessment of player contribution. It also explains how teams can make better selection and retention decisions.

Evaluative Scales

In order to classify the players in accordance with the player categories it is necessary to establish a set of evaluative scales for each of the four measurement areas: accomplishments, professional skills, citizenship values, and leadership. Once each player is placed in a category, it will be possible to determine the composition of each team at each level of the organization. The current composition of each team (superstars, stars, and solid citizens) can be compared to the requirements for winning.

ACCOMPLISHMENTS

5 = Superstar (Hall of Fame): Greatly exceeds past and current players' accomplishments.

4 = Star: Exceeds accomplishments of current players and some past players.

3 = Solid Player: Exceeds average or typical player's accomplishments for the position.

2 = Player: Equal to or below some accomplishments of the typical player in the position.

1 = Oddball: Below the level of the typical player.

PROFESSIONAL SKILLS

5 = Superstar (Hall of Fame): Greatly exceeds past and current players' professional skills.

4 = Star: Greatly exceeds professional skills of current players.

3 = Solid Player: Exceeds average or typical players' professional skills for the position.

2 = Player: Equals professional skills of the typical player in the position.

1 = Oddball: Below the level of the typical player in the position.

CITIZENSHIP COMPETENCIES

5 = Superior Citizen: Greatly exceeds behavioral expectations in every competency area; consummate role model.

4 = Outstanding Citizen: Exceeds behavioral expectations in every competency area; a role model.

3 = Good Citizen: Solidly meets all competency expectations.

2 = Citizen: Meets most competency expectations.

1 = Poor Citizen: Does not meet most competency expectations.

LEADERSHIP SKILLS

5 = Inspirational Leader: Team will follow under the most difficult circumstances.

4 = Motivational Leader: Actively and constructively supports team goals; gains support from others to reach team goals.

3 = Facilitative Leader: Supports the management, captain, and team; may influence others in a constructive way.

2 = Passive Troublemaker: Quietly resists constructive efforts for improvement from management, captain, and other team members; a silent disruptive force.

1 = Active Troublemaker: Openly challenges management, captain, and teammates; a significant threat to team unity and a highly disruptive force.

It was clear in our research that the various Yankee assessors did not weigh all the competencies the same. Bob Fishel told me that he believed that historically the Yankees assessed accomplishment equal to the weight of all the other success characteristics combined. Based on Fishel's input, different weights can be surmised for each competency.

CATEGORY WEIGHTS

Accomplishments	6
Professional skills	3
Citizenship behaviors	2
Leadership skills	1

Utilizing this assessment model (competencies and scales, player classifications and weights), Babe Ruth and Lou Gehrig, Yankee teammates whose careers overlapped, can be hypothetically classified.

				BABE RUTH			

CATEGORY	WEIGHT	MINIMUM SCORE*	TOTAL	RUTH SCORE	TOTAL RUTH SCORE	GAP
ACCOMPLISHMENTS	6	3	18	5	30	+12
PROFESSIONAL SKILLS	3	3	9	5	15	+6
CITIZENSHIP	2	3	6	1	2	-4
LEADERSHIP	1	3	3	1	1	-2
TOTAL			36		48	+12

*Ideally, a minimum score of 3 is required in each competency to qualify for the team.

Babe Ruth was a dangerous oddball because he represented many of the wrong values and was a disruptive force to his teammates. He had an uneven profile, exhibiting strong positives and equally strong negatives. He precipitated battles with ownership, management, and his teammates. He was a challenge to manage. His behaviors might have prevented the Yankees from winning more World Championships. Examples of bad incidents include: suspensions for fighting, fines for breaches of team rules, womanizing, and physical disorders probably created by alcohol consumption and poor eating habits.

While Ruth set the Yankee standard of performance, Gehrig exemplified the Yankee Way. He was titled the Pride of the Yankees, a standard of behavior and bearing that goes beyond wins, losses, and statistics. Gehrig was the Yankee prototype for overall excellence. While Ruth helped launch the dynasty with his bat and charisma, it was Gehrig who solidified it.

Gehrig was a superstar with super-stalwart qualities. He had a career shortened by illness but his statistics attest to his accomplishments. In 1927, the year Ruth hit 60 home runs, Gehrig was selected

American League Most Valuable Player. Ruth won one World Championship before Gehrig and three with Gehrig for a total of four. Gehrig won three additional championships with Joe DiMaggio on his team for a total of six.

			LOU GEHRIG			
CATEGORY	WEIGHT	MINIMUM SCORE	TOTAL	GEHRIG SCORE	TOTAL GEHRIG SCORE	GAP
ACCOMPLISHMENTS	6	3	18	5	30	+12
PROFESSIONAL SKILLS	3	3	9	5	15	+6
CITIZENSHIP	2	3	6	5	10	+4
LEADERSHIP	1	3	3	5	5	+2
TOTAL			36		60	+24

When the talent classifications, based on the hypothetical ideal distribution cited earlier, are applied to an extended 40-person team, there might be two superstars and four stars, with the rest being solid players; there would not be any oddballs.

ROSTER OF A DYNASTY	
SUPERSTARS	2
STARS:	4
SOLID PLAYERS	34
ODDBALLS:	0

We have presented the hypothetical Yankee four-part classification structure and five evaluative categories used to place players in each group. Any organization can learn from this approach by defining in a simple way the most important elements of dynastic success in its industry and developing a suitable rating scale to evaluate and classify its employees. This enables the organization to determine the composition of its workforce and compare it to its requirements, such as those outlined in the "Roster of a Dynasty" chart. A classification chart like the "Roster of a Dynasty" can be built for any organization.

In addition to the actual assessments made on the basis of current conditions, assessors (management, coaches, scouts, and players) can forecast player potential in terms of the same dimensions. A hypothetical assessment of Derek Jeter in his final year as a minor league player illustrates the projection of a star into a super-stalwart.

DEREK JETER			
CATEGORY	CURRENT SCORE	PROJECTED SCORE	GAP
ACCOMPLISHMENTS (6)	24	30	+6
PROFESSIONAL SKILLS (3)	12	15	+3
CITIZENSHIP (2)	8	10	+2
LEADERSHIP (1)	4	5	+1
TOTAL	48	60	+12

Another example of a hypothetical talent assessment follows for Johnny "Big Cat" Mize, a fading superstar, before he joined the Yankees as a part-time star.

The chart on Mize articulates the types of assessment decisions that management, scouts, coaches, and other players make on all players at all levels. Although his ratings dropped when he joined the Yankees, Mize was still close to star level.

JOHNNY MIZE

CATEGORY	CURRENT SCORE	PROJECTED SCORE	GAP
ACCOMPLISHMENTS (6)	30	24	–6
PROFESSIONAL SKILLS (3)	12	9	–3
CITIZENSHIP (2)	6	6	0
LEADERSHIP (1)	3	4	1
TOTAL	51	43	–8

The current and projected classification scores are used to reconstruct the player roster to develop a bench strength summary (succession plan), a concept that is explored more fully in Chapter 8. The organization must also define its key positions. In baseball these are pitcher, relief pitcher, and catcher. The organization must ensure that these positions, once identified, have at least star quality individuals and also must ensure that these positions have backups that are at least potentially star quality.

BENCH STRENGTH SUMMARY

CLASSIFICATION	CURRENT ROSTER	PROJECTED ROSTER	BENCH GAP
SUPERSTARS	2	1	–1
STARS	4	2	–2
SOLID PLAYERS	34	36	+2
ODDBALLS	0	1	+1

Four of six current players who are classified star and superstar occupy four key positions: two starting pitchers, one relief pitcher, and one catcher.

The projected roster has a gap for one superstar pitcher, one star pitcher, and one star catcher. There is a surplus of two solid players. The oddball player should receive coaching and development.

Subsequent chapters discuss how the Yankees use their intuitive classification system to strategically select, develop, and allocate resources to players.

LESSONS FOR YOUR TEAM

How to implement the "Create a Balance of Superstars, Stars, and Solid Performers" principle:

1. Be realistic. No organization can be comprised solely of superstar employees. By definition only about 2 percent to 4 percent of employees fall into this category. You need at least one superstar, though.

2. Create a talent management model to incorporate and describe your employee talent management composition based on your employee classifications.

3. Assess employees on their retention and attraction value, not solely on the basis of their accomplishments and professional skills. Include citizenship and leadership competencies in the assessment.

4. Use multiple assessments of employees against established competencies. This will improve the quality of employee assessments.

5. Select and retain current and projected employees who fit your talent model.

6. Determine your key positions and fill them with employees who can be classified as superstars or stars. Your key positions must have backups that have superstar or star potential. If your organization does not have internal backups, it should recruit externally.

7. Hire fading superstars and stars who are divested from other organizations. They can supply needed short-term professional skills and be role models for citizenship and leadership at lower costs.

LESSONS FOR YOUR TEAM *(Continued)*

8. Be wary of employees who have superior accomplishments and professional skills but fall severely below organization expectations in citizenship and leadership behaviors. They may have short-term value but they can also destabilize the organization in the long term. Make sure dysfunctional talent is on a short leash, reined in when necessary, and let go quickly when their conduct becomes too disruptive.

CHAPTER

8

Establish Your Talent Strategy and Fill in the Gaps

This chapter describes how the Yankees use talent classifications (superstars, stars, solid players, oddballs) to build a comprehensive inventory of players inside and outside the organization. The inventory enables the Yankees to implement a unique three-part strategy:

1. *Identify and retain superstars in their organization and/or acquire them from competitor organizations.*

2. *Ensure the battery (key positions) has at least star and potential star backups.*

3. *Make certain that everyone on the team is rated as at least a solid player.*

This strategy first took shape in the Jacob Ruppert era. This chapter discusses how it has evolved and how the Yankees implement each step of the strategy to guarantee that they field the most competitive team possible.

The Evolution of a Strategy: Part I—The Superstar

In the early years of the Yankee organization, there was no formal farm system from which to draw talent. Owners were dependent on

their relationships with other major league team owners to purchase
or trade for players, or on ambitious scouts who combed the country's
minor leagues, high schools, and colleges seeking to sign talented
young players before their colleagues from other teams offered a competing contract. Owners sought to make the best deal. Sometimes the
Yankees traded their players because of team requirements. Other
times they made moves because of financial considerations. Each
owner unsystematically cataloged the players on competitor teams
and looked for opportunities to steal their most valuable assets.

Jacob Ruppert had seen the Red Sox with Babe Ruth's towering
presence win more than their share of World Series between 1912
and 1918. He also observed the success of other teams, like the Giants, during that time, and soon came to the conclusion that a team
could not sustain such results without a superstar. Ruppert also knew
that Harry Frazee, the owner of the Red Sox, in previous years was an
active and triumphant participant in player piracy. Frazee frequently
purchased high-quality players from other less financially stable
teams. Frazee was able to win championships with these players, but
soon his payroll became unaffordable. His problems were further ag-
gravated by other less financially shrewd business enterprises. The result was a full-scale monetary crisis. To make matters worse, Babe
Ruth, his petulant superstar, was compounding the problem by making unrealistic salary demands. Frazee knew that to retain ownership
of the Red Sox and keep his sanity, he needed both more funding and
to get rid of Babe Ruth. By accomplishing these objectives he felt he
could keep his ballpark and rebuild his team. Ruppert, in a Machi-
avellian moment, came to Frazee's aid. He bought Babe Ruth and
gave Frazee a loan for his ballpark. The acquisition of Babe Ruth left
an indelible mark on the Yankees and baseball. Ruppert now had his
superstar. He would continue to trade and purchase talent to fill in
the gaps on the existing team.

Ruppert also recognized that he needed more than superstar players to win championships. He needed superstar management. He cast his eye in the direction of successful Red Sox manager Ed Barrow. He was impressed by Barrow's winning attitude and managerial skills. He made Barrow his general manager. It was Ed Barrow who understood how to fully optimize Ruth's skills and how to build a team around him. Barrow moved Ruth from an excellent pitcher who played every fourth or fifth day to a daily outfielder and hitter. Ruth had excelled as a pitcher, but his bat was too potent a weapon to have on the bench 60 percent to 70 percent of the time. The Yankees initially saw Ruth's potential to be their much-needed superstar, but through changing his position Ruth emerged as baseball's quintessential superstar. The first step in the talent strategy had been completed.

The acquisition and success of Babe Ruth and Ed Barrow are testimony to how well Ruppert understood the criticality of utilizing superstars and building a team around them.

The Evolution of a Strategy: Part II–Key Position Players

Ed Barrow recognized from his experience with the pitching performances of the Red Sox World Series teams that pitchers were responsible for a disproportionate contribution to the team's success. He also recognized the need to integrate the pitcher's activity with that of teammates on the field. Barrow concluded that the catcher's position was essential to assuring the effectiveness of the pitchers. Miller Huggins concurred with his general manager when he said, "A good catcher is the quarterback, the carburetor, the lead dog, the pulse taker, the traffic cop, and sometimes a lot of unprintable things, but no team gets very far without one."

The Yankees had found their superstar; now they needed to en-sure that they had star talent in the pitching and catching positions. Again, the Yankees turned to the Red Sox and Frazee's financial woes. Barrow traded with the Red Sox for pitcher Waite Hoyt and catcher Wally Schang. The two turned out to be the needed improvements to bring the Yankees their first pennant in 1921. The next year Barrow pilfered two more pitchers from the Red Sox. Joe Bush and Sam Jones helped lead the Yankees to another pennant in 1922. Superstar or at least star level pitchers and catchers are essential for team success. The second element of talent strategy had emerged: Know your key positions and fill them with superstars and stars.

The Evolution of a Strategy: Part III–Solid Players

While the first two elements of the strategy came about under Ruppert in the early 1920s, the final element wasn't fully articulated until the 1940s. Superstars and stars would never constitute the complete roster of any team, including the Yankees. In the 1940s, general manager George Weiss recognized that if the team's roster of superstars and stars was augmented by players who were minimally at the level of their peers on other teams, not just mere warm bodies to send to the plate in be-tween the superstars' at-bats, then the whole team would stay competi-tive for longer periods of time. By comparing the position players with those on other teams and accurately assessing and classifying talent throughout the organization, the Yankees could ensure that their solid players were at the very least comparable to the competition's average players (never below). This strategy is reflected in the development of a farm system (player development) that turns out large numbers of solid players who contribute significantly to team competitiveness.

Developing Structure around the Strategy

In order to implement the three strategies just outlined, the Yankees first needed to evolve tools to convert their talent classifications into an inventory for determining their strengths and developmental needs. The generic baseball name for this inventory is "bench strength summary." It is used by the parent and minor league teams to create charts that list the players by position and talent classification. These classifications are superstars, stars, solid players, and oddballs. The Yankee management and scouts not only make assessments of their players' current categories, they also try to predict players' classifications in one to five years. They do the same exercise for players outside their system.

The parent team and every feeder team in a farm system has a bench strength summary that both describes the current talent inventory and projects the placement of superstars, key position players, and stars into the next level of the farm system. This projection allows teams at each successive level to identify backups and estimates when each backup player would be ready to assume a full-time assignment. These predictions enable the franchise to create a pipeline of talent from lowest minor league team to the parent team. Each organization level is a talent feeder for the next level. The farm system is discussed in detail in the next chapter.

Superstar Strategy

As we saw with the acquisition of Babe Ruth, the first element of the team's three-part strategy focuses on ensuring there are superstars on the parent team and a pipeline of superstars from other sources.

BENCH STRENGTH SUMMARY: SUPERSTAR FORECAST			
LEVEL	CURRENT	NEED	GAP
PARENT TEAM (YANKEES)	4	2	+2
AAA	3	2	+1
AA	0	3	-3
A	2	4	-2

The superstar forecast summary chart is literally a portfolio of players. It indicates that the parent organization might be able to satisfy its need for superstars in the short term but might have a gap in the future. Potential superstars could fill the gap from the farm system, or the parent club may have to rely on external recruitment. Additionally, the lower-level teams in the farm system have higher goals for recruiting potential superstars because not every forecasted superstar will be evaluated at that classification when moved to the next level.

Historically Yankee management and scouts have been good judges of talent. When the Yankees cast their assessments into their bench strength summaries, they are able to determine, beginning with the Yankee major league team, the degree to which they have achieved their targeted talent model. The superstars on the parent team and those in the farm system receive more resources than players falling into the other classifications. These resources include direct pay, recognition, targeted training, development, coaching, and mentoring. This concept is further explored in Chapter 10.

Additionally, it is important to periodically raid the competition for superstars. While obtaining superstars directly from other major league teams is not always possible or desirable at the parent club level, it certainly is a very worthwhile and highly achievable undertaking to pry potential superstars away from competitors' minor league franchises. This not only strengthens the whole organization, but it subtly diminishes the future capabilities of the competition.

Key Positions Strategy

Once the organization has identified and addressed its superstar requirements, it must focus on filling its key positions (pitcher and catcher) with at least star level players. Once again, it does a forecast of its needs.

BENCH STRENGTH SUMMARY: KEY POSITION FORECAST			
LEVEL	CURRENT	NEED	GAP
PARENT TEAM (YANKEES)	4	4	0
AAA	3	5	-2
AA	8	6	+2
A	4	6	-2

The key position forecast supplements the team's superstar forecast. In this hypothetical forecast, the farm system has some gaps in providing long-term replacements for star players in key positions.

Solid Players Strategy

Once the superstars and star key position players are identified, the forecast is analyzed for gaps, and the recruitment methods for filling gaps are determined. Each team in the Yankee system completes the picture by ensuring that everyone on its roster is at least a solid player.

Once again the bench strength summary is used to help ensure that the farm teams and the parent team are fully staffed with the required solid players. To illustrate this point, we have created a hypothetical bench strength summary for the starting 1927 Yankee team. The model includes each player's projected classification in five years and the Yankees' potential backup player from their 1932 roster. The chart also indicates the number of years from 1927 when the player was projected to be ready to move into a position (status).

BENCH STRENGTH SUMMARY: BACKUP STATUS FOR 1927 YANKEES

NAME	POSITION	KEY POSITION?	1927 CLASSIFICATION	FIVE-YEAR PROJECTION	BACKUP	CLASSIFICATION	BACKUP STATUS
Field							
P. COLLINS	Catcher	Yes	Solid player	Solid player	B. Dickey	Superstar	2 years
E. COMBS	Outfielder	No	Superstar	Superstar	L. Lary	Solid player	Indefinite
J. DUGAN	Third base	No	Solid player	Oddball	J. Sewell	Star	1 year
L. GEHRIG	First base	No	Superstar	Superstar	M. Hoag	Solid player	Indefinite
M. KOENIG	Shortstop	No	Solid player	Solid player	F. Crosetti	Solid player	5 years
T. LAZZERI	Second base	No	Superstar	Superstar	J. Saltzgaver	Solid player	Indefinite
R. MEUSEL	Outfield	No	Star	Solid player	B. Chapman	Solid player	3 years
B. RUTH	Outfield	No	Superstar	Superstar	S. Byrd	Solid player	Indefinite
Pitching							
W. HOYT	Pitcher	Yes	Superstar	Star	R. Ruffing	Superstar	2 years
H. PENNOCK	Pitcher	Yes	Superstar	Star	L. Gomez	Superstar	5 years

In 1927, the 10-player Yankee core roster (eight field players plus two starting pitchers) included six superstars, one star, and three solid players. Both lead pitchers were superstars (no formal relief pitcher position had emerged), but the catcher lacked the minimum star classification. Superstars filled four of eight field positions. The Yankees' five-year projected player mix was based on the retention of Combs, Gehrig, Lazzeri, and Ruth because none of the backups were superstar or star level players. The 1932 team had seven superstars—stronger than the 1927 team. The additions came from players on minor league teams. Many baseball experts feel that the 1927 team was the greatest of all time. However, the Yankees went on to win the World Series in 1928, but did not repeat until 1932 when they had seven Hall of Fame players.

The 1932 Yankee championship team had a player mix of seven superstars, one star, and two solid players. The team had two superstar starting pitchers and a superstar catcher. Superstars filled five of eight field positions. The incredibly talented 1927 and 1928 Yankees were even more formidable in 1932. Ironically, after 1932 the Yankees did not win another World Championship until 1936; then they reeled off three more in a row, won in 1941, and again in 1943. The 1936 team had six Hall of Fame players; of the six, Bill Dickey, Joe DiMaggio, Lou Gehrig, and pitcher Lefty Gomez were career Yankees. Tony Lazzeri spent his entire career with the Yankees except for two seasons with other clubs in the twilight of his playing days. Pitcher Red Ruffing was acquired from the Red Sox but had been barely a solid player in his six plus years in Boston. Ruffing emerged as a superstar in his 10 years pitching for the Yankees.

Perhaps the most critical addition to the Yankee dynasty after Gehrig was Bill Dickey in 1928. He was a superstar catcher in a key position. He was subsequently named to 11 All-Star teams and participated in eight World Series. Dickey's replacement, Yogi Berra, participated in nine World Series. A superstar in a key position will make a disproportionate contribution to building a dynasty.

The reserves or bench players on these Yankee teams were typically at least solid players and/or fading superstars and stars. Many of these reserve players would have been starters on less competitive teams. The Yankees are especially adept at finding and attracting such players.

1998 Yankees: A Balanced Winner

The Yankees have fielded many great teams over the past 80 years but the 1998 team had more wins than even the great 1927 team. In fact, to win the World Series, the 1998 team went through two competitive championship series before it could even qualify for the World Series. Let's look more closely at this team. We have once again taken the liberty of doing our own player classification.

PLAYER ROSTER: 1998 YANKEES

NAME	POSITION	CLASSIFICATION	SOURCE OF RECRUITMENT
SCOTT BROSIUS	Third base	Solid player	Oakland
CHAD CURTIS	Outfield	Solid player	Cleveland
DEREK JETER	Shortstop	Superstar	Yankee farm
CHUCK KNOBLAUCH	Second base	Solid player	Minnesota
TINO MARTINEZ	First base	Star	Seattle
PAUL O'NEILL	Outfield	Star	Cincinnati
JORGE POSADA	Catcher	Star	Yankee farm
DARRYL STRAWBERRY	Designated hitter	Star	Minor league
BERNIE WILLIAMS	Outfield	Star	Yankee farm
Pitchers			
DAVID CONE	Pitcher	Star	Toronto
ANDY PETTITTE	Pitcher	Star	Yankee farm
MARIANO RIVERA	Relief pitcher	Superstar	Yankee farm

This team had one superstar, five stars, and three solid players among the starting lineup. It also had a solid pitching staff with several starting pitchers who were stars (two are shown here) and a relief pitcher who was a superstar. The catcher was a star. People might quibble with some of our evaluations, but this team clearly was not filled with superstars. The 1998 team also had a bench of solid players and potential stars. The team boasted five players from the Yankee farm system in the starting contingent. The leader of the 1998 team was the homegrown Derek Jeter.

The Yankee three-part player strategy for the entire dynasty is illustrated in the Appendix. The chart lists the managers, superstars, and star and superstar key position players (pitchers and catchers) for all championship teams.

Any organization can develop such summaries as those provided here. Making these summaries as part of your talent strategy will put your organization on the road to building its own dynasty.

LESSONS FOR YOUR TEAM

How to implement the "Establish Your Talent Strategy and Fill in the Gaps" principle:

1. Classify all your employees (use superstar, star, solid performer, and odd-ball or any terminology that works for your company).

2. Prepare an inventory from the employee classifications to determine whether your company's composition fits organizational needs.

3. Continually identify and build your organization around superstars. Make certain that there is never a shortage.

4. Identify the key positions in your organization. Ensure that the key positions have at least stars and at least star backups.

5. Identify gaps for backups and initiate a recruitment or development process to fill these positions.

6. Ensure that all employees are at least solid performers (i.e., at least comparable to peers in other organizations).

CHAPTER

9

Create a Solid Farm System:
Train and Develop Your People

Since 1929, one of the primary reasons for the continuation of the Yankee dynasty has been the farm system. In the farm system, minor league teams feed talent through the organization up to the parent club, the major league team. During this process, young talented players are developed, their skills are honed, and they learn the values of the Yankee organization. A strong farm system can cost-effectively build its superstar and star base and even trade surplus talent to fill its voids. Continual talent development protects an organization against competitor raids and makes it less susceptible to being held hostage to excessive salary demands. This chapter looks at how the Yankee organization has continually brought new players into the farm system to maintain a steady stream of talent to the major league club.

History of the Farm System

Branch Rickey, the brilliant baseball executive, stated, "Luck is the residue of design." In line with this philosophy, Rickey believed that baseball was a discipline, and that highly competitive players could best be cultivated for a major league team through an organized, rationalized, and efficient internal system of talent identification, development, and placement. In the 1920s, major league teams had few systematic processes for the selection and development of talent. Some teams owned other teams in smaller cities, but none had the infrastructure of one or several other teams whose sole purpose was to develop talent to feed to the major league team. In 1925, unable to outbid the rich clubs, Rickey decided to grow his own talent for the St. Louis Cardinals and put his philosophy of player development to the test. The result was the farm system now considered an essential aspect of any major league team's success. The Cardinals would win five pennants in nine years, and when Rickey left in 1942, the Cardinals were the most successful team in the National League, with a farm system covering hundreds of players on several teams.

The antecedents of farm systems are nearly as old as organized baseball. As far back as 1884, the major league Boston Beaneaters owned a team aptly called the Boston Reserves in the minor league called the Massachusetts State Association. The Reserves were intended to serve as a source of replacements for injured members of the major league team. During the next decade, several major league clubs recognized the value of ready replacements and operated comparable reserve teams. They were viewed, however, more as speedy sources of substitutes than as developmental vehicles for players. They did not represent a well-designed system for preparing players for a career in the major leagues.

Branch Rickey's idea was simple yet elegant. Instead of having a single subordinate baseball team to purely supply warm bodies in case a major league team needed fill-ins, he instructed its management to begin teaching and developing players to become talented major leaguers. Rickey also recognized that players had different levels of talent and that this necessitated a managed hierarchical arrangement of feeder teams within which he could place players based on their talent classifications. Rickey would sign emerging talent, and the hierarchy of minor league clubs would develop and retain a continuous flow of players from the lowest-level team to the parent organization. The reserve clause also benefited Rickey's farm system. It ensured that his players could not leave their team, thereby guaranteeing him control of a large number of talented players. Rickey's theory, in part, was that the development of large quantities of players would lead to the discovery of sufficient quality players.

During the early years of Ricky's innovation, when the Cardinals were discovering, signing, and developing a steady stream of players at little expense, other major league clubs were conducting business as usual. While Rickey's farm system was holding down the payroll for his own organization, the prices for high-quality players were increasing more rapidly for other teams.

At the baseball meetings in 1929, Jacob Ruppert declared that "No ball club could afford the prices being paid for minor league players." He was referring to players from minor league teams that were not part of a major league farm system. A cheaper method of player acquisition had to be found, and Ruppert and many other owners were rapidly becoming aware of the value of Rickey's innovation. It was abundantly clear that the farm system was the most efficient method of acquiring talent for a parent team. Throughout the 1930s, major league organizations began establishing farm clubs. Those that were the slowest to implement a farm system were the least successful in the 1940s.

The Farm System

Every major league team has a farm system that focuses on the enhancement of players through acquisition, assessment, training, and development. Similar to grade levels in a school system (elementary, middle, and high schools) these feeder or minor league teams are classified as rookie, A, AA, and AAA. A prospect can move one level from rookie to A and from A to AA, and sometimes skip to AAA if the player is gifted and put into an accelerated program.

Most A-level players have relatively little experience and have recently been drafted by a major league parent organization through a lottery-style method that pulls its talent pool from high schools, colleges, and foreign leagues. Most AA teams feature potential stars refining their skills. AAA-level players are just under the major league level and are often used to fill in on major league teams if an everyday player goes on the disabled list or is unexpectedly traded. The major league clubs pay the salaries of their farm players and help with some equipment and travel expenses. Minor league team owners are responsible for the rest of the operating expenses.

A primary difference between farm teams and major league teams is the minor league's emphasis on player training and development. Winning, in theory, carries less weight in the minor leagues than player development, though team owners and managers want to have winning teams. Winning minor league teams attract more fans, and this means more profit to the team owners. However, players who are dominating their league are unequivocally moved up to the next level team, which sometimes makes it difficult for farm teams to maintain a winning record.

A Training Ground

The farm system is where the parent team introduces, trains, and develops players based on its recipe for success. For a farm system to work it must have an empowered director (head of talent management), an organizational philosophy (expressed as a code of conduct), clear assessment standards, competent talent scouts, competent managers and coaches, and specific methods for training and development. It is important to institutionalize these processes so that the organization is not dependent on an individual or group of individuals to make idiosyncratic judgments at different points of time. Some experts believe that Rickey's failure to create a dynasty in St. Louis was linked to his inability to create an organization that was not reliant on his own brilliant but fleeting tenure.

The Yankee Farm System

The Yankees entered the farm league business in 1929 when they purchased Chambersburg in the Class D Blue Ridge League. Two years later, they purchased Newark, an International League team. The next year the Yankees made their most significant hire; but it was not a player. It was the appointment of a baseball executive named George Weiss to manage their minor league interests. As discussed in Chapter 6, George Weiss, experienced in successfully developing farm teams, laid the foundation for running Yankee farm teams. He was astute at selecting outstanding scouts, giving them ample budgets, and empowering them to sign prospects. Weiss brought potential talent into the farm system, developed them, retained the best, and sold off the surplus to finance later acquisitions. Weiss established the cycle of returning profits from player sales back into the farm system to ensure a steady stream of high-quality talent.

The Yankees not only develop the professional skills of the players in their minor league clubs, they develop their citizenship and leadership skills as well. All players who come through the Yankee farm system are immersed in Yankee culture. They learn what behaviors on and off the field are expected, and are helped to understand their role in contributing to team winning.

The Yankee farm system currently consists of six feeder teams. There is one rookie team (Gulf Coast Yankees), three A teams (Charleston Riverdogs, Staten Island Yankees, and Tampa Yankees—Advanced A), one AA team (Trenton Thunder), and one AAA team (Columbus Clippers). A farm director guides the system. He acts much like a combination of school superintendent and corporate senior executive for human resources planning and development. He guides the assessment, development, and placement of players.

Most minor league players never progress to the major league level, and like many of their corporate counterparts spend their careers with the same company at the same level—or even when moving to another company still perform the same job. They are solid players at lower levels, with limited potential for upward mobility. Other players, like Mickey Mantle, are scouted right out of high school and spend only a short period of time in the minor leagues. Mantle blossomed quickly in the minor leagues, and in his second season Tom Greenwade, the astute scout who signed him, declared Mantle almost ready for the major leagues. At the end of the 1950 season, the Yankees brought Mantle up to the Yankees from the minor leagues, not only to play but to observe how to behave in the Yankee Way. By 1951, Mantle had been converted to an outfielder from a shortstop, and was on his way to becoming a legend. In 1952, when Joe DiMaggio retired, the Yankees named Mantle their starting center fielder. The continuity of superstars contributed to the team's continued success.

Other Yankee success stories were drafted out of colleges. Thurman Munson was drafted right out of Kent State University and spent two impatient years in the minor leagues. In the 1970s, Munson would be one of the premier catchers in baseball, a determined clutch hitter, and a Yankee role model for his teammates.

The farm system has served the Yankees well, especially in developing outstanding catchers, a key position. Four Yankee catchers, all homegrown, dominated the Yankee dynasty. The Yankees drafted Bill Dickey, Hall of Fame Yankee catcher from 1928 through 1946, from the farm leagues in 1928, one year before the Yankees' own farm system was established. He played his entire career, including eight World Series, in pinstripes. The next three Yankee catchers came through the Yankee farm system and with the exception of Yogi Berra, who played four games with the New York Mets, spent their entire careers in Yankee uniforms. Yogi Berra, also a Hall of Famer, followed Dickey as Yankee catcher. His tenure with the Yankees ended in 1963 with 10 World Championships and 14 trips to the postseason. Thurman Munson served as Yankee catcher from 1969 until his untimely death in 1979. Munson was on two World Series championships and three postseason teams. Current Yankee catcher Jorge Posada has been on four winning World Series teams and been to the postseason 10 times since joining the team in 1995. Twenty-four of the 26 Yankee World Series teams were represented by only four catchers. This is just one example of how the farm system has directly contributed to the Yankee dynasty. It also bears testimony to how occupants of a key position can contribute to the continuity of success.

Assessing Farm System Talent

It is one thing to institute and organize a farm system, and it is quite another to leverage it for available talent to benefit the parent organization. Branch Rickey may have pioneered the organizational structure of the farm system, but the Yankees have perfected finding, assessing, and promoting talent from it.

Historically, the Yankees have used a variety of statistical categories when evaluating the accomplishments and professional skills of their players. The judgment of what categories to use is related to the rules, context, and availability of talent during a particular era. For example, Casey Stengel emphasized hitters who did not hit into double plays, infielders who could make double plays, pitchers who had the opponents hit into double plays, and home run hitters. This combination made his teams fast, powerful, and defensively sound. These criteria were used for selecting and developing players throughout the farm system during the Stengel era. Other managers valued different statistics and measured players by how many runs they drove in or other standards. While these criteria changed from team to team, the Yankee approach for assessing a player's current level of skill and potential for upward growth (accomplishments, professional skills, citizenship, and leadership) remained constant. This allowed managers and coaches at the major league club to create a talent map of each level of the farm system. They knew both the current level of play of all the players at every position at all four minor league levels, as well as the measured potential of all players at all levels. Utilizing this knowledge they created a pipeline of players ready to assume each position at each level of the organization.

Additionally, the parent organization could foresee potential talent problems much earlier than with other systems. The Yankee talent map indicates players moving upward who can replace players at higher levels with no current backups (called voids); surpluses (positions with more than one backup); performance issues (players to be trained, developed, or terminated); and blockages (players preventing more qualified replacements from moving up). Armed with this information, a staffing and development action plan is developed for each team in the farm system with the ultimate goal being the continuation of the Yankee dynasty. The plan will seek to have the correct mixture of current and future superstars, stars, and solid players designated for a 5-to-10-year period. The plan also identifies the requirements and timing to fill each position, as well as the surplus of talent that can be used for trades to fill voids. Historically, the Yankees have been most successful when the farm system generates talent surpluses that can be traded to other teams.

Let's look at a few illustrative individual player assessments to get a better idea of how the Yankees assess talent in their organization. These assessments are made by managers, scouts, and coaches. Each player's developmental plan is incorporated into the bench strength summary of his current team and that of projected teams. It is reflected in current accomplishments and competencies and in level of readiness for moving to higher-level teams. Before assessing a player, let's examine representative players' scores for different classifications. These are shown in a hypothetical chart, based on the classifications previously developed (current and projected) for all players in the farm system.

CLASSIFICATION OF PLAYERS BY COMPETENCY SCORES
(CURRENT OR PROJECTED)

LEVEL	ACCOMPLISHMENTS RANGE	PROFESSIONAL SKILLS RANGE	CITIZENSHIP RANGE	LEADERSHIP RANGE	TOTAL SCORE
SUPERSTAR	30	15	6–10	3–5	54–60
STAR	24–29	12	6–10	3–5	45–56
SOLID PLAYER	18–23	9	6–10	3–5	36–47
ODDBALL	Below 18	Below 9	Below 6	Below 3	Below 36

A hypothetical Yankee assessment for Lou Gehrig while playing in the farm league, one year before joining the Yankees, is shown.

HYPOTHETICAL LOU GEHRIG CLASSIFICATION

COMPETENCY	CURRENT LEVEL	POTENTIAL LEVEL	WEIGHT	SCORE	MINMUM REQUIREMENT	GAP
ACCOMPLISHMENTS	5 Superstar	5	6	30	18	+12
PROFESSIONAL/ TECHNICAL SKILLS	5 Superstar	5	3	15	9	+6
Hitting						
Fielding						
Throwing						
Running						
Knowledge of rules						
CITIZENSHIP	5 Superior citizen	5	2	10	6	+4
LEADERSHIP	5 Inspirational leader	5	1	5	3	+2
TOTAL	5 Superstar-Stalwart			60	36	+24

Also shown is a hypothetical developmental profile of a solid player on his way to becoming a star.

HYPOTHETICAL JORGE POSADA CLASSIFICATION

COMPETENCY	CURRENT LEVEL	POTENTIAL LEVEL	WEIGHT	SCORE	MINIMUM REQUIREMENT	GAP
ACCOMPLISHMENTS	3 Solid player	4 Star	6	24	18	+6
PROFESSIONAL/ TECHNICAL SKILLS	3 Solid player	4 Star	3	12	9	+3
Hitting	3 Solid player					
Fielding	4 Star					
Throwing	4 Star					
Running	4 Star					
Knowledge of rules	3 Solid player					
CITIZENSHIP	3 Solid player	4 Outstanding citizen	2	8	6	+2
LEADERSHIP	3 Solid player	4 Motivational leader	1	4	3	+1
TOTAL	**3 Solid player**	**4 Star**		**48**	**36**	**+12**

DEVELOPMENT ACTIONS:
  Play in winter league against better competition to build credible accomplishments.
  Hitting: Change batting stance; work with hitting coach; special timing drills.
  Citizenship: Allow opportunities to sign autographs and mingle with fans; encourage to be upbeat even in slumps.
  Leadership: Encourage providing suggestions on team improvement; mentor a rookie player.

The Farm System and Spring Training

The Yankees are renewed each year during the rites of spring training. It is an event that breathes life into the team's talent assessment and development charts. It is a unique opportunity for players from the previous year's parent team to join with upwardly mobile players from the farm system and acquisitions from other teams to collectively hone their professional skills and reenergize the winning culture.

Spring training is where members at all levels of the organization, but in particular "farmhands," can assess their current competency levels, further enhance areas of strength, work on areas for development, share experiences, and learn to work better with current and future teammates. The players eat, live, and train together in a contained environment. Spring training is baseball's equivalent of a so-called corporate university, but it was conceived long before the idea germinated in the mind of some innovative corporate training director.

No one is precisely sure of the genesis of spring training. Somewhere in the haze of myth and folklore baseball historians seem to agree that it took root before 1900 and began to flourish in the 1920s. The Yankees were said to have begun spring training activities as early as 1901.

The idea of spring training became tangible when teams began to build, lease, or rent permanent training facilities in Florida. Soon afterward spring training quarters became year-round centers for player training and development. The Yankees' facility in Florida is appropriately called Legends Field. It is a 31-acre complex that seats 10,000 people with the same dimensions as Yankee Stadium. The complex is replete with memorabilia and its own Monument Park that honors the great Yankees of the past. The physical character of Legends Field is a constant reminder of the Yankees' winning tradition.

During spring training Legends Park is staffed by top professional skill instructors, coaches, and tacticians who help players and managers assess developmental needs and hone skills. This intellectual capital is complemented by superb equipment that enables players to translate their knowledge into game-related activities. The combination of intellectual capital, state-of-the-art training equipment, and a facility imbued with the spirit of winning is a powerful brew for success.

Subsequent to the workouts of early spring training, players participate in games first against teammates and then against competitors. These games are the Yankee equivalent of so-called corporate training simulations. They enable the players, managers, coaches, and scouts to provide greater assessment and developmental recommendations to improve player performance.

Corporate "spring training," extended periodic happenings that bring together several organization levels in a controlled environment, can result in personal improvement for all participants and invaluable planning information for the organization. As in baseball, spring training can revitalize an organization's charts for replacements, and supply input for training and development programs.

Customized Training and Development

In order for players to advance through the farm system, they must have personal improvement programs that meet their specific needs. These improvement programs must be carefully customized and delivered by qualified coaches and instructors employed by the team. Additionally, current and former team captains, superstars, and stars can serve as mentors and assist the formal training and development team. Experienced players are expected to provide mentoring to players who have recently joined the team. Ongoing input and advice on the Yankee Way form an integral part of both citizenship and leadership competencies for all players.

The goal of training and development is to continually provide players with experiences, coaches, and mentors that will enable them to minimally exceed the average accomplishments of peers in the same position. Frequently, injured major league players undergo rehabilitation at a minor league affiliate. The farm teams ideally should take advantage of this situation by having the major league player provide input and mentoring to minor league players while he is recuperating.

The farm team's training and development goals are similar to the goals of corporate learning centers where employees, after assessment of developmental requirements, receive the proper training to excel at their present position or move to a position at a higher level in the organization.

Remove Blockages for Your Stars and Superstars

The success of a farm system, in the corporate world as well as in baseball, is predicated on the removal of blockages for emerging stars. The various levels in the organization must continually make room for new stars and superstars to move up so that their skills can be continuously challenged and improved. Often fading stars are blocking an emerging star. In traditional organizations, elimination of fading stars and superstars through termination may not be possible unless their accomplishments slip below standards. The organization must think creatively to redeploy them into jobs that make better use of their coaching, mentoring, and professional skills. One of the toughest problems faced by an organization is the replacement of falling stars and superstars with rising ones, but it must be done for the long-term viability of the company. Since the whole company is a farm system, there must be a continual flow of talent from the lower to higher levels.

The key to long-term organizational success is to make good evaluations and then to have the discipline to implement the model based on the assessments. For most of the Yankee dynasty, the assessments of players have been made by excellent scouts, coaches, and managers. Talent assessment and management from the farm leagues through the parent club has been a key source of Yankee differentiation.

LESSONS FOR YOUR TEAM

How to implement the "Create a Solid Farm System" principle:

1. View each organization level as a part of a farm system where employees are recognized early in their careers, developed to their optimal abilities, and moved to higher levels in the organization as positions become available.

2. Have an executive with authority and credibility who charts all employee assessments, recommends training and development plans, establishes career paths for employees, and tracks backups for all key positions.

3. Make the needs determination derived from the talent assessment process the basis for each employee's development plan.

4. Use talent assessments to create a "bench strength summary" for your entire organization. The bench strength summary indicates surpluses (positions that have more than one replacement for an incumbent), voids (positions with no replacements), blockages (positions with nonpromotable incumbents in the path of high-potential employees), problem employees, superstars, and star employees.

5. Allow for emerging talent to replace fading talent. Creatively use the experienced employee to enhance the company while ensuring that emerging talent is not blocked along their career paths.

6. Make sure that proper assessments of all employees have been conducted in a fair and disciplined way and that investments made in employees are consistent with their talent classifications and developmental needs.

7. Consider initiating a corporate university that includes intellectual capital, state-of-the-art developmental tools, and a facility that reflects a winning tradition.

CHAPTER

10

Pay Your People Based on Their Contribution to Organization Success

Babe Ruth said, "Someday every player will be paid his true worth." Ruth's words finally rang true with the death of the reserve clause. Today a player's salary should be based on his current and projected talent classification as a gauge of his actual and potential contribution to the team. The Yankees use this assessment of contribution as the basis for making decisions on the salaries of players on their major and minor league teams and prospective players from a myriad of other sources. In order for this approach to be effective, the team must have accurate player assessments and a detailed knowledge of specific talent requirements. The latter typically comes from an organization-wide bench strength summary and talent management plan. Twice in their history, for extended periods of time, the Yankees failed to follow this disciplined approach. The result each time was a large payroll and mediocre team performance.

Most organizations cannot afford to spend payroll dollars haphazardly. Missteps can lead to inability to attract star talent or, even worse, loss of your top people to competitor organizations. For this reason, your organization must remember that the first principle in compensation management is not spending more than you can afford. The second principle is spending what you can afford wisely. Whatever your budget, wisely spending your money is the key to sustainable competitive success.

Baseball's History of Unfair Pay Practices

For most of baseball history player compensation was arbitrarily determined by capricious, self-serving owners and senior managers. The players had little recourse since they were bound to their teams by the infamous reserve clause. Some owners even allowed their general managers to personally retain a portion of player payroll if they came in under budget. Many owners and general managers cruelly took advantage of this type of cost-containment incentive offering to literally cheat accomplished players out of their due compensation. Players were well aware of this practice, and the result was heightened antagonism between management and players. Worst of all, players were at the mercy of owners when it came to performance rewards; typically the owners were not very generous. The infamous Black Sox game-fixing scandal was reputed to be instigated by unfulfilled ownership pay promises to players. Babe Ruth consistently fought with Harry Frazee, the Red Sox owner, and Jacob Ruppert, the Yankee owner, over pay for performance issues. In 1959 Mickey Mantle's $70,000 contract contained a provision that $10,000 would be withheld until the end of the season. The money would be released only if, in the judgment of the Yankees, Mantle had lived up to "team rules."

The Yankee owners, until the reserve clause ended in the Steinbrenner era, were among the most notorious abusers of equitable and meritorious player compensation practices. Other than fairness and integrity, why would the callous owners make any adjustments in pay since player movement between teams was at their discretion and there was no open, competitive pay market? Was there any inducement for owners to provide increased rewards to players? The answer to this question was a qualified, limited, and painful "yes." The owners were literally forced to make adjustments to pay for the following reasons:

- *Holdouts*. Superstar and popular players would not report to spring training, thereby potentially jeopardizing their performance, destabilizing team performance, and agitating the fans and media. Joe DiMaggio and Babe Ruth, among others, pursued this course of action.

- *Poor morale*. Bob Fishel told me that one year after Mickey Mantle won the American League triple crown (home runs, batting average, and runs batted in), a rarely accomplished feat, George Weiss, the Yankee general manager, tried to cut his pay by 20 percent. Weiss told Mantle that although his batting average increased and Mantle was the league's Most Valuable Player for the second straight year—and the Yankees won another American League championship—that he would take a pay cut because his home run and runs batted in production had declined from his previous year's numbers. Mantle was reduced to tears. It was only after Stengel, Fishel, and other Yankee executives interceded on the basis that Mantle's morale (and performance) would be lowered did Weiss back off. Many years later, Mantle, responding to a question regarding what his pay would be like if he was currently playing, said, "I'm not quite sure but I would back up a Brinks truck to Mr. Steinbrenner's office and tell him to keep shoveling until no more money could fit in the truck." Other superstars like Yogi Berra and Whitey Ford had similar experiences with the Yankee front office.

- *Disregard of rules*. Babe Ruth signed a lucrative contract to barnstorm around the country with a few teammates and semipros on the "Babe Ruth All-Stars." Baseball banned such tours by World Series participants. Major League Baseball and the Yankees believed that barring World Series participants from barnstorming increased the players' dependence on World Series money and, in theory, provided an incentive to win. The barnstormers were fined the amount each earned in the World Series and suspended for lengthy periods.

- *Airing dirty laundry.* Players challenged the manager and owner by publicly making their case for a pay increase. This embarrassed the Yankee organization and created external pressure to support the player. Babe Ruth, Joe DiMaggio, and Mickey Mantle engaged in this practice.

The Yankee management viewed player requests for salary increases as a form of insubordination. There is, therefore, little that we could or should learn from the Yankees' early history regarding employee compensation other than the fact that as managers we need to put in place professional programs to avoid the types of employee reactions such as those just described. It's no defense of Yankee ownership to note that between 1920 (Babe Ruth's acquisition) and 1975 (the hiring of Catfish Hunter) they were on a par with other teams in their harsh compensation treatment of players.

Before free agency there were gaps in payroll size between the teams with a large fan base and those with a small fan base. In the days before television and radio rights and the preponderance of commercial products, team incomes were dependent on ticket sales. The larger cities, like New York and Chicago, were dubbed "big market teams" and were thought to have a competitive advantage over the "small market teams" like Detroit and Cleveland. Visiting teams did share in the revenues of their hosts on the road. The Yankees were the most popular and/or hated team and drew the most fans on the road. Yankee ownership did not spend these earnings proportionately on pay and therefore the team was highly profitable. From the 1940s on the Yankees derived a real competitive advantage through their investments in their wildly successful minor league organization—the tap that produced a reservoir of cheap talent. The dynamics of player pay changed dramatically when the reserve clause was terminated.

Today the financial gap between "have" and "have-not" teams has grown, with the Yankees squarely installed as the leader of the haves. But it is not the mere expenditure of money that wins championships, certainly not 26 of them over 80 years. The Yankees have been successful because they have identified and retained talent within and outside of their organization. While many teams spend money foolishly on players who are poor matches with their organizations, the Yankees, for most of their history, have been adept at selecting the talent that would be the most beneficial to their organization and paying that talent accordingly. We learned in previous chapters how the Yankees find and assess talent. Now let's look at how they pay that talent.

Player Assessment and Compensation

As discussed in Chapter 9, during the assessment stage, players are classified by their actual and potential contribution to the team. These classifications should take into account accomplishments, professional skills, citizenship, and leadership skills, and each player's pay level should be based on these current and potential contributions.

The player market is comprised of about 86 to 88 percent solid players, 10 to 12 percent star players, and only about 2 to 4 percent superstars at any given point in time. Each category represents a player's retention or acquisition value, and the player's compensation package must correspond to this value. If a team loses or cannot acquire a superstar, especially one in a key position, the potential effect can be extremely detrimental to the team.

A competitive team must first allocate sufficient resources to attract and retain superstar players. Similarly, star players are also valuable assets, and although they are somewhat more plentiful than superstars, their retention value is sometimes only slightly less significant. The last group to be considered is the solid players. Solid players should be fairly compensated with the remaining payroll budget. Solid players have a lower retention value to the team, are typically less attractive to competitors than superstars or stars, and may be less likely to move from a championship team to one that is less competitive because of small financial incentives. They are also much easier to replace than superstars or stars. The Yankees' farm system has produced a rich trove of solid players, and occasionally a resource-poor competitor has been willing to take several of them in exchange for a single star because the competitor believed the trade would strengthen its overall team capability.

Basing Pay on Contribution

Let's first look at the relationship between pay and classification for three levels of players (superstar, star, and solid player) using their actual and potential contribution to the team as a basis for a pay decision.

RECOMMENDED PAY PACKAGES BASED ON CONTRIBUTION

	POTENTIAL CONTRIBUTION		
CURRENT CONTRIBUTION	SOLID PLAYER	STAR	SUPERSTAR
SOLID PLAYER	Moderate	High	Very high
STAR	Minimal	High	Very high
SUPERSTAR	Minimal	High	Very high

The grid provides guidance to management in making a decision on the magnitude of a player's compensation package. The strongest combination of player classification (retention value) will yield the highest levels of compensation. The terms in the grid refer to the relative size of the pay package compared to the pay of a reference group of players (sometimes called a benchmark sampling).

In the corporate world, this type of grid can serve the same purpose as in the baseball arena. Managers should allocate employees' pay based on a hierarchy of retention value (current and projected contribution to the team).

Companies cannot afford to lose, or fail to acquire, stars with superstar potential and superstars who are projected to maintain their superstar accomplishments. These vital contributors must be the first consideration in establishing salary guidelines. Their pay packages fall into the very high category. Once these salary packages are in place, the pay packages for stars and potential stars are determined. Although the loss of these people is less of a blow to the company than losing a superstar or potential superstar, it would still be a major setback. These salary packages, too, must ensure that stars are appropriately paid so that they will not seek employment elsewhere or fail to be acquired by the team. Their pay packages are set high. Solid performers who are projected to stay solid performers or a superstar who is projected to have diminished accomplishments (become a star) should be compensated fairly and in line with peers.

Finally, players who are projected to be reclassified from superstar or star status into solid performers due to diminished accomplishments no longer make the same high level of contribution they formerly made. Furthermore, they could be blocking a more qualified player from ascending to a higher level. When pay levels for these players are not adjusted for diminished contribution, the team no longer is getting its money's worth from the fading player. This practice bloats payrolls and ultimately leads to poor team performance. The most likely remedies for players falling into this zone are trade, termination, pay freeze, or reduced pay.

Baseball teams have more leverage with players in this last situation than corporations have, because the players are under fixed-term contracts and not subject to many of the usual labor laws. The teams will likely try to trade these players while they have some value to another team. Falling stars and superstars may have more value to other teams because even their diminished accomplishment levels exceed those of current players, their charisma may bring more fans (customers) to the ballpark, and their professional, citizenship, and leadership competencies may set an example for the behaviors of other players. The key is to trade these players while they are still attractive to another team and to pursue emerging stars at lower compensation levels. Elston Howard, in the waning years of his star level career with the Yankees, was traded to the Boston Red Sox during one of the Yankee dark ages when the Yankees were attempting to rebuild their team with younger players. Howard provided citizenship and leadership to a contending team. The Red Sox got to the World Series. Howard made his contribution, although short-lived, to the competitive legacy of the Red Sox and the Yankees.

Similarly, management should also take into consideration the life cycle of employee accomplishments before allocating pay in accordance with the grid. Obviously, a current star with superstar potential and a 10-year window for accomplishment has more retention value than a comparable star with only a three-year window, and should be paid accordingly.

The basis for all comparisons is the competitive rates for each player's salary based on their accomplishment level. Teams can compare their players against a range of compensation factors. Let's look at an example for the first base position.

	CLASSIFICATION OF COMPETITOR'S TALENT		
FIRST BASEMAN	**SOLID PLAYER**	**STAR**	**SUPERSTAR**
AVERAGE SALARY	$1 million	$5 million	$10 million
BATTING AVERAGE	.250	.295	.330
AVERAGE RUNS BATTED IN	65	80	145
AVERAGE NUMBER OF ERRORS	15	9	3

SALARY SURVEY FOR FIRST BASEMAN

The team can then appropriately determine a range of pay utilizing the competitive data and their own assessment of their own player's actual and potential contribution level using the classification grid previously described. They may also modify their pay determination based on key position status, strong citizenship, and high leadership.

A Pay Premium for Key Position Players

The next judgment to be made is whether a player's position is key to a team's success. In baseball, the case can be made that for all teams there are four key positions: catcher, two starting pitchers, and a relief pitcher. During recent Yankee dynasty years, the Yankees have emphasized acquiring superstar or star level pitchers. The Yankees understand the old maxim stating "Good pitching will control good hitting." Taking this maxim a step further, a good catcher can enhance good pitching.

At least star quality players who meet at least the minimal requirements of citizenship and leadership must staff key positions on a competitive team. Low talent availability at key positions further reduces the size of the available talent pool and fuels higher levels of competitive pay. Because of this, a premium is paid for players in key positions. Pay for star players in key positions is typically forced into the highest levels even if they are not superstars.

A compensation survey of players in key positions on other teams provides a benchmark for establishing a potential pay level for the Yankee superstars and key players. The Yankees are prepared to pay premium rates (well above the average) to put a player in a premium position or to protect them him being pirated by another team. One way they have historically minimized the pain of high payments is to move someone up from their farm system who has the potential to be a superstar or star in a key position. Although a premium is paid for potential, it is relatively low because achievement has not yet been realized. Once a player's potential is realized, the team must pay the former farmhand an accomplishment premium or risk losing him to a competitor.

The key element of player compensation strategy should be to pay the minimal salary to the right player in the right position based on assessment of contribution. When assessments are incorrect and/or the pay model just discussed is not followed, the team staggers under a payroll that does not reflect player value.

Determine Competitive Pay for All Positions

Every team needs to know the level of competitive pay for each of its positions before it can determine the correct pay package for players occupying these positions. Baseball teams have easy access to the competitive pay levels and statistical accomplishments of every player on every team. The executive office may even be able to obtain from scouts and players the citizenship and leadership values of players in competitive positions. All baseball executives and players have the advantage of actually watching competitive players perform. In the corporate world this information is not as publicly and easily available, but it can be collected informally through contacts with potential employees in association meetings and conferences, from references, and from candidates themselves. Organizations can obtain competitive salary information from surveys performed by compensation survey companies, consulting firms, government agencies, and other professional and credible sources. They should use this data, rather than anecdotal data provided by recruiters, to make salary decisions. It would be inconceivable for a baseball team to determine a potential player's pay package simply on the basis of a scout's intuitive sense of competitive pay for a selected group of players.

When the Yankees take a long-term view of their players' pay, they must reconcile projected rates for benchmarked competitor players with the forecasted performance of their players. If the forecast is wrong, the result could be excessive compensation or player dissatisfaction over perceived inequities.

Poor Investments Lead to Failed Performance

Anyone who believes that throwing money at talent guarantees success should look closely at Steinbrenner's dark age of 1982 to 1994. There were no visits to the postseason series during this period, and the team was largely uncompetitive despite liberal spending on players with ostensibly strong capabilities. This era was characterized by poor assessment of talent, inefficient leveraging of the farm system, and a failure to follow the historic staffing model. The result was the over-payment and misuse of talent, reduced fan attendance, and uncompetitive performance. In the 1990s, Yankee performance sank to the lowest level since 1913, yet the payroll was higher than those of competitors. There was no vast public outcry to "break up the Yankees" from detractors. Only Yankee fans relished this possibility.

Because of their wealth, the Yankees have been able to fund mistakes that would cripple other teams. The majority of teams cannot afford missteps so they have to spend even more wisely with smaller margins for error. For this reason competitor teams must be better at classifying talent and applying pay more appropriately than the Yankees. They must remember that the first principle in compensation management is not spending more than you can afford. The second principle is spending what you can afford wisely. Whatever your budget, wisely spending your money is the key to sustainable competitive success. How your payroll is distributed is a function of your determination of what positions are key, your assessment of your players' actual and potential contributions to the organization, and your ability and discipline in linking pay to these classifications.

Incentive Pay

In Major League Baseball, the principal purpose of compensation is centered on attracting and retaining players in a fluid, limited, and highly competitive market. This function is served by guaranteed pay. A secondary purpose is to get players to focus on other types of accomplishments that are important to the team. Sometimes these accomplishments are covered under the provisions of guaranteed pay, but increasingly they fall under an evolving set of nonfixed pay opportunities called incentives. These additional elements can include All-Star and World Series appearances, Most Valuable Player awards, number of games played, number of games pitched, and ranking in key categories.

The growing sophistication in developing critical performance measures helps teams implement incentive programs. Three conditions enable teams in their implementation of incentive programs. These are:

1. The team is able and willing to identify critical success measures.

2. The team is able to use a specific annual performance period.

3. There is credible data that could be used to compare player performance with an identified reference group of competitive players.

There remains a critical requirement, however, that is difficult to achieve: a high degree of player control over results. Players do not have adequate control of intangible elements to achieve their prestated goals. Managers must be free to utilize players based on game requirements, thereby potentially limiting game appearances. Injuries can limit playing time. Outsiders vote for the Most Valuable Player, making the selection very subjective. The performances of other players directly influence a player's performance, thereby affecting his statistical rankings and his prospects for appearing in a World Series.

An individual's ability to control his destiny is a key requirement for establishing an incentive pay plan. Inherent in baseball incentive plans is an inability to allow for this requisite. For most players, therefore, the incentive plan will not be the engine that drives performance. Certainly management and the player are aware of this fact, and it is no coincidence that the largest component of pay is typically guaranteed, with a smaller portion targeted to improvements or special achievements.

What are the true incentives for professional players once an equitable and competitive guaranteed pay level is reached? They appear to be nonmonetary! First is the player's desire to win and to be recognized for his professional skills. Successful Yankee players are driven to compete in postseason play at a minimum and ideally in the World Series. They want to be treated as professionals and play with other professionals. They want to play for a team whose ownership and management are committed to winning. Therefore, a player's work environment is the best motivation beyond appropriate pay levels. This is as true in the business world as in the baseball world.

LESSONS FOR YOUR TEAM

How to implement the "Pay Your People Based on Their Contribution to Organization Success" principle:

1. Know what you can afford to spend on employee pay and spend no more. Every organization, no matter how wealthy, has a finite amount of dollars for salaries.

2. Base employee pay on actual and potential contribution to your organization.

3. Base employee pay on competitive pay practices for comparable positions in organizations with which you compete for talent.

4. Take every step to ensure that every employee's talent classification is accurate.

5. Pay should first be budgeted for attraction and retention of superstars, with stars as the second consideration.

6. Pay solid citizens equitably based on the competitive market for a representative group of peers. Solid citizens are less likely to be pirated by competitors, and they are unlikely to leave the organization for small pay differentials. If they do leave, they are more easily replaced than are superstars or stars.

7. Key organization positions must be identified and pay allocated to fill these positions with superstars or stars.

8. Develop your own "farm systems." They are essential for controlling payroll costs.

9. Establish a work environment where employees are motivated by their contributions to organizational success.

CHAPTER 11

Make the Superstar the Focal Point of Your Organization

A superstar is a commodity in short supply. This makes the superstar a very special ingredient in a talent management program. That is why we single this person out for special attention. As discussed in the previous chapter, superstars generally comprise only around 2 percent to 4 percent of the number of players in any given year. Their value to their team is immeasurable. Even without looking at statistics, the superstar's presence alone inspires confidence. When he is absent from the starting lineup due to injury, heads begin to droop in the dugout and mistakes are made on the field. The level of play of the remaining team members is considerably lower when the superstar isn't playing his position. Now imagine if that superstar is out of the lineup for good, lured away by a competitor. Not only is the competition much stronger in that position, but also the original team is leaderless. Talk about competitive advantage.

Hiring your competitor's superstars weakens the direct competitor's strength, demoralizes all competitors, greatly improves your team, and creates media focus that heightens fan (customer) interest. And the Yankees are the best in the baseball world at doing exactly that. Paradoxically, however, the Yankees did not pirate a superstar from a competitor between the 1920s (Babe Ruth and Waite Hoyt) and 1975 (Catfish Hunter). Since then they have used superstar acquisition in a highly selective mode. When the Yankee farm system started to produce high-quality talent, the Yankees added superstar retention to their strategy of superstar acquisition.

The Babe Ruth Effect

In 1914, when Jacob Ruppert and Tillinghast Huston bought the organization, the Yankees were a team with no history of success, mired in the bottom half of their division. The Yankees had no farm system from which to draw talent. They had to find talent wherever they could. The two colonels realized the quickest way to get on the road to fielding a competitive team was to purchase talent directly from competitor organizations. The success of their first acquisition from the Philadelphia Athletics, a star pitcher named Bob Shawkey, encouraged them to continue this practice.

The Athletics, a highly successful team in prior years, were an excellent mark because of their weak financial position. Harry Frazee, the owner of the Boston Red Sox, had savaged the Philadelphia Athletics' roster throughout this era, and he used the Athletics' top talent to build his World Championship teams. Frazee, like Ruppert would do later, preyed on weaker teams because he could afford to. The fragile franchises became the farm teams for the robust organizations. By 1920, the Red Sox themselves had become a fragile franchise. They wouldn't play for another World Championship until 1946.

Harry Frazee, the Red Sox owner in 1920, was much maligned after his sale of Babe Ruth to the Yankees. He is accused of bringing the "Curse of the Bambino" upon the Red Sox.

But the Yankees weren't finished with the Red Sox quite yet. Ed Barrow was Yankee general manager from 1921 through 1939 and upon Ruppert's death became president of the team until its sale in 1945. It should be no surprise to learn that like Ruth, Barrow was lured from the Red Sox to the Yankees. Barrow had been Red Sox manager in 1918 and 1919. He managed them to their last World Championship in the twentieth century. In Barrow's first year as general manager with the Yankees, the Yankees won their first pennant. The Yankees would win six league pennants (championships) in Barrow's first eight years, another in 1932, and another four between 1936 and 1940 as Barrow and George Weiss built up a farm system in the 1930s. Barrow was also responsible for converting Ruth from a pitcher to an outfielder. Ruth had been very successful as a southpaw pitcher for the Red Sox. He was a significant contributor to the Red Sox World Series victory in 1918. But Barrow recognized that Ruth's real talent lay in his home run swing. He needed to be an everyday hitter. Ruth's bat was too potent a weapon to have him sitting on the bench between pitching starts. The first year Ruth was a full-time outfielder he hit 54 home runs, more than any other entire team in baseball.

As in the case of Barrow and Ruth, often high achievers in one organization may become even greater performers in another. The Yankees identified Barrow's executive skills from earlier minor league experiences and hired him as general manager, not as field manager. Barrow had sound field managerial skills but superstar executive abilities. Barrow made sure that Ruth's superstar career as a pitcher and occasional batter was converted into a baseball-transforming full-time position as an outfielder and daily hitter.

The haves' advantage over have-nots is also true in the non-baseball world. Organizations that perform better and are on better financial footing generally pay more and can offer more opportunity to superstar and star level key position employees than less successful organizations are able to. In addition to monetary gain, the corporate equivalent of a superstar in a key position is more likely to want to work for a winning organization. The superstar conveys the aura of winning. The desire of a player or an employee to be associated with a winning organization makes that organization an employer of choice. Employers of choice will be more successful than their competitors at securing topflight talent from competitors and retaining their own key people.

Organizations that bring in their competitors' superstars cannot sit back and assume that the star performer's career will continue on a high performance level. These employees are used to being highly recognized and assured that they have ample opportunities to display their skills. Organizations must develop and communicate clear and exciting career paths that include opportunities to acquire new skills, new growth experiences, and new successes that will continue to strengthen their attractiveness in the marketplace. Superstars must feel they are moving ahead, respected and appreciated as valuable contributors, and fairly compensated for their talents. Once you have attracted and hired your competitors' superior performers, you must ensure that your competitors don't lure them right back. It is, of course, a two-way street.

The Superstar Market

There are very few superstars, by definition, in the talent market. There are even fewer super-stalwarts in the talent market. This makes the recruitment, development, cultivation, deployment, and retention of them integral to sustaining success. A team must find a way to fill gaps in its bench strength plan with actual superstars and star key position players on the parent team and potential ones in the farm system. Every time a superstar player is taken from a competitor, the transfer destabilizes the competitive environment. These teams believe that they have lost some type of competitive advantage—and they're correct. Losing a superstar is a direct threat to the success of the team. Every time a superstar or star key player changes hands, opposing teams attempt to adjust their rosters to remain competitive. This makes for a very fluid market for high-quality talent, and this condition, in turn, spawns higher player compensation.

The Yankees dabbled with superstar acquisition in the 1980s, most notably with future Hall of Fame honorees David Winfield and Ricky Henderson. Unhappily for the Yankees, they played during the second dark age. More recently, the Yankee acquisition of superstar Roger Clemens (by trade) in 1999 led to two World Series victories, four World Series appearances, and five visits to postseason play. Alex Rodriguez, another superstar, came to the Yankees in 2004 via trade, and his accomplishments contributed to a berth in postseason play.

Homegrown talent led the Yankees to two World Championships and a "wild card" postseason appearance between 1996 and 1998. The Yankees knew they must not lose this talent and ultimately paid a high price for its retention. However, it would have been even more financially costly, assuming it was possible, to replace the homegrown talent.

Retention of Homegrown Talent Is a Competitive Advantage: Go to the Marketplace Only When Necessary

Between the acquisition of Babe Ruth and Waite Hoyt in the early 1920s and the start of the free agency era, the Yankees neither bought nor traded for superstars. The Yankee superstars were all Yankee farmhands, players who came up through the Yankee organization.

The list is impressive, including Lou Gehrig, Bill Dickey, Joe DiMaggio, Whitey Ford, Mickey Mantle, and Yogi Berra. The Yankees did trade for or purchase from other teams stars and fading superstars to complete their targeted roster, using a combination of cash and minor league players to make these deals. Sometimes they acquired farmhands from other teams to strengthen their own farm system, but the vast majority of the players in the starting lineup for the Yankees were from within the organization. This allowed the team to cultivate players based on Yankee criteria and also limited the money expended to bring talent to the team. The same principle applies to organizations: It is more expensive to hire a superstar than to develop one.

George Steinbrenner, like the other principal owners who preceded him, was opportunistic. His arrival in 1973 coincided with both the end of the reserve clause in Major League Baseball and the erosion of the Yankee farm system. Steinbrenner promised a competitive Yankee team within three years of taking over the front office. He adapted to a new economic and competitive model by using the new free agency rules to the team's advantage. By contracting with free agents, Steinbrenner could overcome the failure of the farm system to deliver the needed superstars by directly negotiating with free agents to join his team. He acquired Hall of Fame superstars Catfish Hunter in 1975, Reggie Jackson in 1977, Dave Winfield in 1981, and future Hall of Fame inductee Ricky Henderson in 1985. The age of big spending had begun, and no one would do it better than George Steinbrenner; but spending alone produced poor results between 1982 and 1994.

Maximize Your Superstars' Contributions

Not all superstars are created equal. They come in all shapes and sizes as well as personality types. All baseball superstars have superior on-field accomplishments as compared to their peers but many have inadequacies when citizenship and leadership skills are taken into account. We have previously discussed Babe Ruth's and Reggie Jackson's flaws, but other Yankee superstars also had their weaknesses. It is incumbent on the team's managers to recognize their superstar's limitations or idiosyncrasies and to skillfully manage these to the team's advantage. Yankee managers have been adept at leveraging their superstar's limitations. Here we discuss three Yankee superstars whose team contributions were optimized by savvy managers.

The Reluctant Superstar: Joe DiMaggio

Joe DiMaggio had great accomplishments and possessed superior professional skills, average citizenship skills, and minimally acceptable leadership skills. DiMaggio's commitment to daily excellence is abundantly clear in his statement "There could be a kid who may be seeing me for the first and last time. I owe him my best." DiMaggio was supremely confident in his professional skills, but off the field he was a taciturn, socially awkward, and often surly person. He was neither a leader nor a follower and was reluctant to mentor his teammates. Although he was keenly aware that Mickey Mantle, his center field replacement, revered him, DiMaggio never exerted a serious effort to participate in the grooming of "The Mick" to be his replacement.

Casey Stengel was aware that he needed to get more out of his superstar than just on-field performance. But he also knew that the remote and sometimes indifferent DiMaggio would rarely initiate constructive contact with the other players. It is true that he led by example, but the professorial Stengel sought to leverage DiMaggio's strengths for the good of the team. He knew the best way DiMaggio could be utilized was through the sharing of his flawless professional skills and extensive knowledge of the game. He offset DiMaggio's aloofness by assigning DiMaggio as an adviser to emerging players in spring training. Casey told DiMaggio it was necessary for him to instruct other players for the team to win; DiMaggio complied. Additionally, Stengel offset DiMaggio's reticence by surrounding him with other less charismatic players who would use DiMaggio's superstar radiance as a source of energy for helping teammates to strive for winning. Stengel spread DiMaggio's influence through other players. If a player like Old Reliable Tommy Henrich said that DiMaggio wanted an emerging star to try a little harder, the aura of the association with the great DiMaggio worked its magic.

The Beloved, Immature Superstar: Mickey Mantle

Mickey Mantle had great accomplishments, possessed great natural abilities ranging from mercurial fleetness to Herculean strength, and exhibited basic citizenship skills, but demonstrated rudimentary leadership skills. No one will dispute the fact that Mickey Mantle was loved for his warm personality and self-sacrificing and disarming nature. Although he retired after the 1968 season and died at a relatively young age, Mantle is still revered as the most popular player over the past 50 years.

To paraphrase Casey Stengel, "Mantle had more speed than a sprinter and more wallop than a slugger, but less sense than a teenager." Mantle's leadership inadequacies had to be offset to maximize his contribution to team success. Casey Stengel and Ralph Houk, Mantle's managers, were aware of the admiration the team held for him because of his willingness to play in great pain, his loyalty to other players, and sincere good ol' boy demeanor. The managers converted player admiration for Mantle into a team work ethic. They motivated players "on behalf of Mantle" to strive harder to win when Mantle was on the disabled list or playing hurt. The managers also knew that Mickey's own role model was his father, "Mutt," who died before Mickey reached superstar status. Mantle neglected his health with binge drinking, late-night carousing, and other un-healthy activities stemming from his morbid belief that he would die young. The managers filled the void in Mantle's life by becoming "Mutt's" surrogate and providing him with the guidance needed to constructively influence teammates.

The Underestimated Superstar: Yogi Berra

Yogi Berra was known for his uncanny ability to hit in clutch situa-tions and for his folk wisdom. He was a rare commodity—a talented catcher who was a superior left-handed hitter. The great Giant player Mel Ott said, "Yogi could stop anything behind the plate and hit anything in front of it." The average fan knows that Yogi's overall hitting and fielding statistics are among those of the top catchers of all time, but his ability to manage the game from the field level is equal to his mythic accomplishments on the field. However, his comic comments and equally comical appearance ob-scured his on-field accomplishments. Even when he became a major league player, Berra was the butt of demeaning remarks compar-ing him to monkeys. Berra stoically responded, "Aw, nobody wins games with their faces." Only five feet eight inches, Berra was squat and stocky and appeared awkward and slow. Yet he was agile and powerful.

Yankee scouts saw beyond Berra's appearance and signed him for only $500 after other teams backed away. Berra became a team leader through his unique presence and lack of conceit. Berra was a role model for integrity and dignity. His humility and professionalism earned him the respect of teammates and management. He had a constructive and motivational influence on teammates. This influence is evidenced by Yogi's admonition to his team to come from behind to win: "It ain't over till it's over."

Yogi's tactical skills were recognized and used by Casey Stengel, his manager, who proclaimed Berra his field manager. Stengel described Yogi as "a strange fellow of remarkable abilities." Berra's abilities were not even overlooked by Joe DiMaggio, who publicly branded Berra the best field general and tactician in the game. In later years Berra's professional, citizenship, and leadership skills were recognized by the Yankees and the Mets, both of whom made him their manager. As manager, he got both teams to a World Series berth. In response to a question to explain his various successes, Yogi responded by saying, "You can observe a lot by watching."

Continual Recruitment of Superstar Talent

Recruitment of superstar talent to drive a dynasty must be continuous. The organization must constantly court superior people from outside the organization. No one knows when a high-quality talent will get injured, his skills will erode, or, worse, the player will be pirated.

Baseball is not completely a free market when it comes to the freedom of players to move from one team to another. Superstar talent is usually locked up by long-term contracts designed to hold them until their superstar powers start to fade. In the business world, noncompete contracts and long-term incentives are attempts to block highly talented people from moving their skills elsewhere. These hindrances should mean little to a pirating organization since the potential organizational benefits of the superior people far outweigh the trouble of recruiting them.

There are a variety of strategies for obtaining super people. The Yankee strategy starts with an understanding of the competencies required to assess talent for the team. This includes: affirming the four critical aspects of player measurement (accomplishment and professional, citizenship, and leadership skills). With this knowledge, they can enlist everyone as a scout (armed with knowledge of the team's competency requirements). The informal organization-wide scouting apparatus must be supported by a best-in-class system for continually scouting and monitoring actual and potential superior people from other organizations.

The best-in-class scouting system must be run by a world-class scouting director (head of recruitment), a set of professional scouts (recruiters), and supported by everyone else. The formal scouting organization must have a database for collecting information and for classifying and sorting information on candidates suggested by the professional scouts and by the virtual network. Once the system identifies candidates, professional scouts will confirm the qualities of the candidates before recommending them for team consideration. Frequently candidates do not know they are under consideration, particularly if they are farmhands in another team's farm system. After subsequent reviews by the director of scouting, team manager, coaches, and executive management, the player may now appear as a candidate or backup on a bench strength summary.

The team essentially employs a multirater assessment (executives, managers, scouts, and coaches) using its own requirements to classify candidates for inclusion in bench strength summaries.

Sound evaluation is the key to locating and recruiting new superstars to the team.

Building Bridges to the Superstars

The Yankees cannot negotiate directly with players under contract with another team. They can negotiate only when they are free agents. In the business world, we generally do not have this restriction, although noncompete and confidentiality agreements can pose recruitment challenges at executive levels. One of the best ways, however, to build a bridge to superior people is through the existing players, managers, and coaches. When player morale is high, the team has a reputation for a long-term commitment to winning, ownership and management are professional, and the organization has core values, the players can represent a positive franchise image to prospective new teammates. Such satisfied players are the best recruiters. They can also be an invaluable source of information that helps the parent club assess the characteristics and benefits that would attract a potential recruit to signing with the team. Great players want to be identified with a great organization because they believe it will help them further their career accomplishments and ensure that they are winners. Derek Jeter, superstar and captain, has been very effective in convincing good candidates to join the Yankees.

LESSONS FOR YOUR TEAM

How to implement the "Make the Superstar the Focal Point of Your Organization" principle:

1. Track as many as possible of the competitors' current and potential superstars and stars, especially in your key positions.

2. Have a strategy for courting superior people.

3. Make absolutely sure that you don't lose any of your own superior people.

4. Know the best sources of recruitment of superior people.

5. Make it a goal and create special awards for internal scouts who recruit superior people.

6. Use current superior people as recruiters of superior people. Superior people need to feel that they are part of a special cadre of people with whom they are proud to be associated.

7. Manage your superior people to maximize their contributions to the organization.

8. Ensure, through proper career development and pay, that you retain high-quality talent. Continuously monitor the satisfaction of superior people with the mentoring, training, and career development programs offered to them.

PART III

Design Your Culture for Success

CHAPTER

12

Diversify Your Talent Pool

Diversity is a success principle that evolved under George Steinbrenner. Until the Steinbrenner era, the Yankees lagged in expanding the ethnicity of the team. Baseball talent was what intrigued Steinbrenner, not the color of his players' skin. He knew that to fully implement the Yankee talent strategy no group of people could be excluded from the pool of available talent. Eight years after Jackie Robinson broke the color barrier, Elston Howard became the first African-American Yankee player in 1955. The Yankee dynasty was diminished by its failure to consider quality talent from all sources when their competitors were doing so. The failure of the Yankees to expand their pool of diverse players in the 1940s and 1950s reduced the number of superstars and stars available to the team in the late 1960s and early 1970s. This shortsightedness contributed to the Yankees' first dark age from 1965 through 1975. Today the Yankees are a blend of African-American, Latino, Asian, and Caucasian players. This diversity has been translated into on-field and box-office success. There are no restrictions on where they will search for talent. They know that they must search even in the most unconventional places to bolster talent at all levels of the organization.

The Globalization of Major League Baseball

The Yankees opened the 2004 season against the Tampa Bay Bucca-neers in Tokyo. The same year, the Montreal Expos played a signifi-cant percentage of their "home" games in Puerto Rico. These events mark Major League Baseball's recognition of the advantages of ex-panding baseball beyond North American borders. The global growth of MLB is reflected in the growing global community of MLB fans. As foreign players have successfully penetrated MLB, as re-flected in the fact that more than one-third of Major League Base-ball professional players were born outside the United States, baseball fans in many other countries follow the successes of their native sons. Many of these countries have a strong cultural attach-ment to baseball, whether in the form of MLB or local leagues and teams. MLB has for several years been moving to exploit the poten-tial of this growing global community of baseball fans. As MLB notes, "America's pastime is growing—and most of that growth is happening outside the United States." Gene Budig, president of the American League, has asserted that "Our national pastime is now the world's."

The success of foreign players in MLB and MLB's efforts to tap into a global community of baseball fans represent elements in the phenomenon of the globalization of baseball. The business of MLB now involves accessing global markets for: (1) baseball consumers in many countries besides the United States and (2) baseball talent. In going global to access these markets, MLB behaves like other big busi-nesses facing globalization in their respective areas. Multinational companies have for many decades been building global markets for their products and utilizing a global labor pool to manufacture those products.

Seeking Talent through Diverse Channels

Superstars and stars, especially in key positions, are a scarce commodity and there is no shortage of competition for their services. This means that each team must make a strategic commitment to identify and scout a broader range of high-quality people and sources for them. The battle for talent now rages globally. Talent markets are as far-reaching as Japan, Korea, Mexico, Australia, Venezuela, and the Dominican Republic. Within these countries, as in the United States, there are many distribution channels for talent. These unconventional places of yesterday have now become conventional places to search for talent. The Yankees, like most of their competitors, are covering the globe to seek out potential talent.

Within these different talent markets and in the domestic baseball leagues, players undervalued by other teams—like aging superstars, stars, and stars in key positions—can serve as an alternate source of bench strength. They, too, can be useful in staffing the organization with people who can still make a substantial contribution although at a slightly diminished level. These people can assume roles where other talent at a comparable level is unavailable or too costly. The Yankees have been historically successful at finding and correctly deploying such talent.

In the corporate world, these bench strength sources would come under the rubric of diversity. For a long period of time, Major League Baseball, and the Yankees in particular, paid no attention to diversity. Today the major leagues no longer penalize people because of race, national origin, religion, or other extraneous factors. Successful teams will carefully search these sources, precisely assess potential talent, and boldly move to take risks to capture highly qualified players. George Steinbrenner was the first Yankee principal owner to recognize, embrace, and promulgate diversity as a strategy for sustaining the dynasty.

Reasons for Diversity

In order of diminishing importance, a review of the Yankees' behavior since 1975 suggests the following reasons for diversifying their talent horizons:

- Diversification expands the talent base for recruiting superstars, stars, and key position stars. This enhances the team's chances in achieving its staffing model.

- Diversification expands the fan mix. This leads to greater ticket and merchandise sales, broader media attention, larger listening and viewing audiences, and higher advertising revenue. The Yankees recognize that there is a huge actual and potential fan base within and outside American borders that can be tapped through diversity. Japanese fans closely follow Japanese players, Mexican fans track their countrymen, and so forth.

- Diversification provides a variety of thoughts and emotions emanating from varied cultural experiences that enable team members to better share common goals, to investigate alternative solutions to problems, and to weather tough times.

The Yankees' Checkered History of Diversity

Diversity is a success principle endorsed by George Steinbrenner. However, until the Steinbrenner era, the Yankees lagged in expanding the ethnicity of the team.

George Weiss, the person responsible for building the best farm and scouting system in the 1940s, 1950s, and 1960s, was shackled by his own bigotry that prevented him from utilizing the Negro Leagues as a source for introducing black players into the Yankee farm system. Weiss believed that black players could never meet all the Yankee appearance standards. To Weiss, being Caucasian was one of the requirements of being a Yankee. He was also appealing to a segmented fan base. He declared, "I will never allow a black man to wear a Yankee uniform. Box seat holders from Westchester don't want that sort of crowd. They would be offended to have to sit with niggers." As a result of his narrow-minded approach, black players in the farm system were traded and others in the Negro Leagues were overlooked. This meant that star players like farmhand Vic Power never moved to the parent team and Ernie Banks (Chicago Cubs), a future superstar and Hall of Fame honoree, was never considered as a backup for Phil Rizzuto, Yankee Hall of Fame shortstop. Weiss was emblematic of corporate discrimination, bias, and intolerance in post–World War II America.

Yankee principal owners' opportunism enabled them to successfully leverage three tipping points in baseball. However, the fourth tipping point, the inclusion of players from diverse backgrounds, was pointedly ignored. The other three tipping points were:

1. Leveraging the financial instability of competitor owners after World War I. Ruppert realized this in the purchase of Babe Ruth and other quality players' contracts from the Boston Red Sox.

2. Recognizing the importance of developing a farm system just before World War II (Topping/Webb/Weiss), evidenced by the large pools of high-quality talent in the 1940s and 1950s.

3. Aggressively pursuing free agents in the 1970s. Steinbrenner acquired free agents Catfish Hunter and Reggie Jackson.

The Yankees Accept Diversity: Elston Howard

There are several milestones that reflect the Yankees' history with diversity. Several cases clearly illustrate the introduction to the team of minority players, executive management, coaches, and advisers. By 1955, Yankee players would have to be blind not to observe the contribution of black players on teams that had provided their stiffest competition. Local players like Jackie Robinson (Dodgers), Roy Campanella (Dodgers), and Willie Mays (Giants) were making major contributions to their teams. The Yankees slowly began to understand that *any* talented player could help them win, and winning was their first priority. Their motives were far from altruistic, but the result was to accept an outstanding black player on the team. In 1955, Paul Krichell, the astute scout, encouraged the owners to sign Elston Howard. He stated, "Both as a man and as a ballplayer . . . Howard looks every inch a Yankee." Howard represented the initial breakthrough.

Howard's contract was purchased from the Kansas City Monarchs, a Negro League team. Howard's acquisition made the Yankees one of the last teams to diversify their racial composition. When Elston Howard was introduced to the media, he proclaimed, "It's great to be a Yankee," thus echoing the acclamation of several generations of white predecessors. But Howard had a difficult time. During his first five years on the Yankees, Howard was the only player without a roommate. He was often isolated and was welcomed by few Yankees. Phil Rizzuto, self-appointed team goodwill ambassador, was one of the few to include Howard in off-field activities. Howard referred to Rizzuto as his "Great White Father."

Howard played in his early career under Casey Stengel. Stengel and his coaching staff were men of an earlier time who peppered their talk with politically inappropriate terms when referring to blacks. Howard, like Robinson, always comported himself as a gentleman. He described Stengel in a positive light when he stated, "I don't think Casey Stengel ever cared about your color if you wore the Yankee uniform with pride."

In fact, in everything but his skin color, Howard embodied Yankee pride. He was a good hitter with excellent defensive skills. His accomplishments were admirable enough to win him an American League Most Valuable Player award, nine appearances in All-Star games, and two Gold Glove awards (defense). He played in nine World Series with the Yankees and one with the Boston Red Sox. He contributed to the Yankees' winning four World Series and was the catcher (key position) in two of them. His ability to hit in the clutch enhanced his level of respect with teammates and fans, who expressed admiration for him. This admiration was the primary source of his leadership. He understudied superstar Yogi Berra until 1960, when he formally moved into the key catcher position. In his attire, Howard had the refined appearance of his Yankee teammates. He was always neat, polished, stoic, and respectful. Because he embodied every aspect of the Yankee Way, "Ellie" commanded the respect of the Yankee pitchers and he was considered a field general for the entire team.

Although the Yankees were years away from fully embracing diversity, Howard became the role model not only for future Yankee

African-American players but also for all Yankee players. He was in the mold of traditional Yankee legends like Tommy Henrich (Old Reliable) and Lou Gehrig (The Iron Horse), who displayed all the required Yankee competencies. He was a Yankee to his teammates and fans.

Slow Shift to a Diverse Team: The Dynasty Stumbles

Over time, the Yankees became integrated, but as late as the 1962 World Championship team they had only two African-American and two Hispanic players. In 1963, Al Downing became the first African-American pitcher in Yankee history. He was only the fifth African-American player on the team.

After 1964 the Yankees did not appear in a postseason game until 1976. There is little doubt that this failure was linked to the practices of the 1940, 1950s, and 1960s when the scouts were still not recruiting and the farm system was not cultivating players of color. The Yankees lacked a clear and definitive philosophy and strategy for embracing and sourcing a diverse team that met the Yankees' four major requirements—accomplishments and professional, citizenship, and leadership skills. Elston Howard clearly exceeded the requirements in all categories. He was a highly successful star-stalwart player in a key position (catcher). He was a bright light in the baseball firmament. However, the Yankees failed to leverage Howard's reputation in instilling diversity as a team success strategy. Howard was a token black player.

As a star and role model, Elston Howard was ultimately brought back to the Yankees as a coach and mentor for emerging players after his retirement as a player. He served in this role for 11 years. He was able to provide a linkage to the winning legacy by his professional skills and by his ability to communicate the myths, folklore, and lessons of the past with great dignity. He helped facilitate postseason play in the volatile competitive era of 1976 to 1981. The team needed more black role models like Elston Howard but the farm system was not growing them.

Diversity under Steinbrenner Bears Fruit

In 1996, Bob Watson became the Yankee general manager and the first African-American to achieve this high a position for the team. Watson was a former star player with a long and successful career on several teams. He played for the Houston Astros for 14 years before moving to the Red Sox and then the Yankees. He was a member of the Yankee 1981 American League championship team. He was highly respected by players, management, and fans. His most outstanding traits were fairness and discipline. Before becoming general manager of the Yankees, he held a similar position with the Houston Astros. Watson, like Howard, fit the Yankee profile of accomplishment, professional skills, citizenship, and leadership. His appointment ushered in the era of some of the greatest Yankee teams. Every year between 1996 and 2004 the Yankees have been in postseason play. They have also appeared in six World Series through 2003. Joe Torre, a manager in the tradition of Huggins, McCarthy, and Stengel, was selected at the start of Watson's reign. Derek Jeter, half African-American and future Yankee captain, garnered Rookie of the Year honors in Watson's first year.

Watson's career with the Yankees, although relatively brief, prepared him for the job of vice president for on-field operations in the commissioner's office. Watson is a role model for all of baseball.

Grooming an African-American within the Yankee Structure

Willie Randolph played on Yankee championship teams from 1976 through 1981. Randolph was assessed as a potential star by Yankee scouts when he was part of the Pittsburgh farm system. They pursued him and he quickly became an integral part of the dynasty. He became a star player who also exemplified the Yankee tradition of quiet pride, accomplishment, professionalism, citizenship, and leadership. He was the first African-American Yankee captain. He returned to the Yankees after retiring as a player to serve under Joe Torre as a field coach and most recently as bench coach (the manager's principal adviser). In 2005, Randolph was selected to manage the New York Mets. He is a great role model in the tradition of the true Yankee legends. He is a quiet leader who produced in the clutch and had the respect of his teammates.

Hispanics Have a Significant Presence on the Yankees

Latinos have made their mark on Major League Baseball, with the Yankees being no exception. Baseball is popular in Hispanic countries, and some small countries like the Dominican Republic have produced a bevy of talented major leaguers. In the early 2000s 20 percent of the players in the majors and 40 percent of all players are Latinos. Hispanics are also immigrating to the United States in record numbers. In 2003, almost 40 million or 13.7 percent of the U.S. population are of Hispanic descent. Hispanics outnumber African-Americans in the U.S. population by almost 1 percent and their numbers are increasing.

As recently as 10 years ago the Yankees had three Hispanic players on their roster. The 2004 team boasted 13 Latinos covering all positions. The list includes superstar relief pitcher Mariano Rivera from Panama, pitcher Orlando "El Duque" Hernandez from Cuba, star catcher Jorge Posada from Puerto Rico, and star outfielder Bernie Williams from Puerto Rico. Rivera, Posada, and Williams have spent their baseball career to date with the Yankees. They are all Yankee-developed farmhands. The Yankees realize that scouting, signing, and developing Latino players is a key to long-term dynastic success. Furthermore, Latino players attract their own fan base to the ballpark, and with the growing number of potential Hispanic fans, it is also good business sense to have Latinos on the team.

Even Fidel Castro could not block the Yankees from recruiting stars. "El Duque" Hernandez defected from Cuba to Costa Rica in 1997. In doing so he became a Major League Baseball free agent. The Yankees moved quickly to obtain his services and were rewarded by his stellar performance during the regular season and exceptional postseason play.

Luis Sojo is a Hispanic solid player-stalwart who had two stints with the Yankees as a second baseman from 1996 to 1999 and 2002 to 2003. Sojo's qualities—his work ethic, support of ownership, amiable personality, ability to garner respect from teammates and fans, and ability to hit in the clutch—were clearly evident in his statement of joy after contributing the crucial hit in the final game of the Yankees' twenty-sixth World Championship. Sojo said, "Today is the happiest day of my life. . . . They [the Yankees] gave me a chance to come through." He, like many of his Hispanic peers, is a great role model. His clubhouse presence is so positive and compelling that the Yankees asked him to succeed Willie Randolph as a field coach in 2003.

It appears that the future for Hispanic players on the Yankees and in Major League Baseball is very rosy. Only seven Hispanic players have been enshrined in the Hall of Fame to date, but they likely will have plenty of company in the years to come.

Embracing Japanese Superstars and Stars

Japanese baseball dates back to the 1870s, almost as far back as American baseball. Japan's first pro team formed in 1920. Casey Stengel's All-Stars went to Japan in 1922 to compete against their Japanese counterparts. Lou Gehrig and Babe Ruth, among other American players, went to Japan to demonstrate their outstanding skills. There has been a long connection between American and Japanese baseball, but one that was not leveraged until recent times.

Japanese baseball has not made it easy for American teams to pirate their players. Under a 1998 U.S.–Japan agreement, American teams must bid for the right to negotiate only with Japanese players who have received permission from their teams. One such player was star player Hideki Irabu. George Steinbrenner became enamored with Irabu when the Japanese pitcher insisted that he wanted to play only for the Yankees after his Japanese team negotiated a contract for him with the San Diego Padres. Ultimately the Padres released him and the Yankees signed him for a hefty sum. Although he played a relatively short period of time with the Yankees, Irabu's presence expanded the Yankee Japanese fan base. Irabu also set the stage for other Japanese players to join the team.

Currently the Yankees have a Japanese player on their roster. Hideki Matsui was a premier slugger for the Yomiuri Giants. He was a superstar on a team that dominates Japanese baseball so completely that it dwarfs even the Yankee influence on the game in the United States. Matsui's former team claims one of every two Japanese baseball fans. Typically Japanese fans are angered by the move of one of their star players to the American major leagues. Their anger was turned to pride when Matsui's performance clearly contributed to two postseason and one World Championship appearance. Matsui probably would not have abandoned his Japanese team for any American club other than the Yankees.

Matsui, with his unparalleled work ethic and unglamorous ways, is the paragon of Japanese virtue that correlates with Yankee pride in many ways. For nine years, Matsui labored industriously for the Yomiuri Giants, never missing a game despite a variety of injuries. Matsui's streak of 1,250 consecutive games is the second longest in Japan. He also stayed a low-key nice guy, always ready to accommodate his adoring Japanese fans with an autograph. He is a living memorial to the words of Yomiuri Giant founder Matsutaro Shoriki, whose deathbed wish was, "May the Giants always be strong, and may they always be gentlemen." These words could have been uttered by Jacob Ruppert and still ring as the prototype Yankee.

Age Diversity and Reclamation

Teams can benefit from mature players who still have the potential for great contributions and can stand as role models and mentor their younger teammates. Baseball is a young man's sport, but balancing a team with a span of maturity levels can provide a healthy mix of ideas and emotions. The Yankees have historically given aging players a second chance to leave their mark on baseball.

Johnny Mize is a prime example of a superstar player in the twi-light of his career who made major contributions to the Yankees. The first baseman slugged 359 career home runs, hitting three in a game six different times. Mize was one of baseball's great sluggers. His ac-complishments earned him a spot in the Hall of Fame. After a long career with the Cardinals and Giants, "The Big Cat" joined the Yan-kees in mid-1949 as a part-time first baseman and full-time pinch hit-ter. Not only did he contribute his professional skills to the Yankees, but his mature leadership and mere presence were an inspiration to his younger teammates.

Another aging superstar Hall of Fame honoree who contributed to Yankee success is Enos "Country" Slaughter. Slaughter was a con-sistent hitter who enjoyed a 16-year career with the St. Louis Cardi-nals before coming to the Yankees. He played on two World Championship teams with the Cardinals in the 1940s. In the 1950s Slaughter contributed to three Yankee pennants. Slaughter was the epitome of hustle. His reputation as an aggressive, smart player who relished winning and taking the extra base inspired his younger Yan-kee teammates.

The Yankees have also reached out and embraced star players with checkered careers who were considered too troublesome by other teams. These players added another dimension to the team di-versity and revealed a humanistic side to Steinbrenner's character. Steinbrenner signed troubled slugger Darryl Strawberry, a former New York Met, in 1995. Strawberry, endowed with enormous talent, had become a star with the Mets but due to drug and alcohol abuse never realized his full potential. His career appeared to be over when no club picked him up, but he signed with the independent minor league St. Paul Saints and proved to Steinbrenner that he could still play. Steinbrenner insisted that he be re-signed. Strawberry provided enormous power as a hitter and was an inspiration to his teammates for his grittiness in fighting adversity. He had remained drug free, with regular testing by Major League Baseball. Strawberry had his best season in seven years in 1998 but the next year he was diagnosed with colon cancer and again encountered drug problems. Steinbrenner gave Strawberry another baseball opportunity in 2003, naming him the team's Player Development Instructor. "I'm very excited to be back with the organization," said Strawberry. "I thank The Boss for this opportunity to work with young players." Early in 2004 Strawberry left the Yankees to work for his church in community and youth outreach.

Dwight Gooden was a teammate of Darryl Strawberry on the Mets who also had substance abuse problems. Gooden set a major league rookie record for strikeouts with the Mets. Gooden became the Mets' ace and helped make them an overnight contender. He was the youngest All-Star ever. Gooden reached new heights in 1985, winning the Cy Young award, which recognized him as the most outstanding National League pitcher for the year. He was on his way to baseball immortality. However, in 1987 Gooden went into a drug rehabilitation program before the start of the season and although returning to the Mets did not have the dominating accomplishments of his early years. The Mets sent Gooden to rehab several times over the following seasons and in 1994 Commissioner Bud Selig suspended him for the rest of 1994 and all of 1995. With a year and a half off from organized baseball between 1994 and 1996, Gooden persevered in his determination to pitch again. He defeated his inner demons, and was given another chance when George Steinbrenner signed him in 1996. Gooden made the most of the opportunity, hurling a no-hitter against the Seattle Mariners on May 14, 1996. Subsequently several physical problems caused Gooden to not be re-signed, and he went to other teams before being given yet another chance with the Yankees. Gooden played in the minor leagues in 2000, was brought up to the Yankees toward the end of the season, and performed well for the eventual World Series victors. After this stint with the Yankees, Gooden retired.

George Steinbrenner's Impact on Yankee Diversity

The diversity initiatives under George Steinbrenner added a new dimension to the concept of team. A new Yankee principle emerged. It postulated that the team would be strengthened on the field and in the dugout and be more attractive to a broader fan base if the ethnic and racial background of the team was varied. The Yankees would not compromise a player's need to meet base levels of the four Yankee requirements—accomplishments, professional ability, citizenship, and leadership skills. Steinbrenner made diversity a fifth qualification. Sound business practices and alternative points of view broadened the perspective of the team and made it stronger financially and on the playing field. Diversity became an integral part of the talent management program. This meant the sources of recruitment were expanded, with scouting taking on global dimensions.

In addition to expanding the sources of recruitment under Steinbrenner, the Yankees had to address cultural issues that might interfere with assimilation into a winning team. The front office and coaching staff has done a good job in instilling Yankee pride into its multicultural players—they all wear the pinstripes with dignity. All players, regardless of the culture from which they come, must be well groomed according to the historic Yankee image. Interestingly, the assimilation of players regardless of heritage has gone smoothly due to the combination of correct player selection, Yankee folklore, and a staff adept at modeling expectations.

Joe Torre appears to be the right manager for a multicultural Yankee team. He was raised in Brooklyn, known as a melting pot, and has the sensitivity that such a background develops. Multicultural players have appeared to adapt well to the team requirements and appear to communicate well with their teammates regardless of language. Somehow a winning team has its own language and the multicultural players learn the winning vernacular very quickly.

The Yankees and Major League Baseball Reach Out

Recognizing the need to support and encourage minority involvement, Major League Baseball is promoting diversity through ongoing programs that reach out and respond to a diverse cross section of the community. MLB encourages minority participation at all levels of the game. It has developed a Diverse Business Partners Program that encourages women-owned and minority-owned businesses to do business with the leagues. MLB has also recognized the contributions of the Negro Leagues to baseball by establishing a pension fund for former players, supporting the Negro Leagues Museum, awarding Jackie Robinson Foundation Scholarships annually, and supporting symposia to sustain baseball programs at black colleges. It also sponsors the Major League Baseball Urban Youth Initiative, whose purpose is to cultivate diversity in all aspects of the game, to provide recreational activities for urban youth, and to prepare minority high school players for college and professional baseball programs.

The Yankees have embraced opportunities to reach out to minority populations. A 2003 event honored the top New York City students of Hispanic descent as determined by their teachers and principals. The honorees were recognized before their families and Yankee fans at Yankee Stadium prior to a game. During the festivities, Yankee pitching ace Mariano Rivera received the Latino Sports Person of the Year Award for his commitment to the Hispanic community. The Yankees understand how such events translate into good marketing practices.

Yankee Success at Diversity

Although the composition of Yankee teams becomes more and more diverse, the basic tenets that have sustained the Yankees throughout its dynasty still prevail. They include:

- Understanding the principal goal—winning a World Championship and the personal benefits that come with a World Series ring.
- Selecting players who already meet or will meet Yankee competency requirements.
- Respecting other players.
- Recognizing that all teammates are evaluated according to the same measurement standards.
- Helping in the recruitment of other multicultural and minority players.

LESSONS FOR YOUR TEAM

How to implement the "Diversify Your Talent Pool" principle:

1. Ensure that management goals for diversity are connected with policies that lead to a diverse cadre of employees.

2. Expand sources of recruitment.

3. Ensure that other employees look for and support employees from a wide assortment of backgrounds that mesh with the core competencies of your organization. Establish this as a citizenship skill.

4. Ensure that all employees understand that employees from diverse backgrounds will contribute to organizational success or will be gone.

5. Ensure that all employees are assessed equally on clearly defined competency measurements.

6. Use members of diverse groups to recruit other members of diverse groups.

7. Have a formal program for introducing and cultivating employees from diverse groups into the organization's culture. This can include written information, group presentations, and assignment of mentors and coaches.

8. Develop community goodwill by sponsoring community events that reach out to minority and multicultural groups.

CHAPTER 13

Celebrate Your History, Heroes, and Legends: Creating Traditions of Excellence

Perhaps no other organization is so filled with myth and legend as the Yankees. The names of the players, their monuments in center field at Yankee Stadium, the retired numbers, the stories, the pinstripe uniform, the World Championship banners, the rings they wear, all of it is part of what people think about when they think about the Yankees. This is not by accident. The Yankee organization has gone to great lengths to promote their history and tradition of excellence. The Yankees tell their stories, publicly celebrate past heroes and legends, and use their past successes to persuade current and prospective players to believe that they are destined to win. The Yankees are more than a team. They are an American success story that has captured the imaginations of people worldwide. On and off the field, the Yankees have been successful at selling themselves. Beginning with the Ruppert era, each primary owner embraced promotional rules.

Use Role Models to Transmit the Team's Legacy

Yankee folklore is transmitted through the principal owner, manager, captain, superstars, and stalwarts of all types. They share the stories and acknowledge past champions. They are the daily reminders of what it takes to be a champion and the custodians of the Yankee Way. The Yankee Way is enmeshed in the team's history and every genera-tion of Yankees builds on the Yankee Way template. Winners write history, and the Yankees have written more than their share.

Every organization has a history, values, and competencies that set it apart and must be consistently conveyed by all levels of employ-ees. Its history, values, and characteristics form its own organization "way." When employees feel ownership for their company "way" they are in a better position to pass on the tradition.

Record the Exploits of Heroes and Legends

There is no other professional sports team that has as many books and articles written about it as the Yankees. Library shelves are filled with volumes discussing the team's history. Even the most inwardly di-rected player has encountered material about the Yankee tradition, heroes, and folklore. The Yankee public relations staffs regularly scan material containing information about the Yankees and may use it in shaping communications to the players. The players cannot avoid reading about the types of physical and behavioral symbols associated with Yankee success.

The Yankees have been blessed with some charismatic super-stars, stars, managers, and owners who through their unique personali-ties have left an indelible mark on Yankee history. Familiar names, like Babe Ruth, Yogi Berra, and Casey Stengel, have become not only Yankee folk heroes but national treasures. Still others with less dynamic personalities have become ingrained in Yankee folklore because of their triumphs in clutch situations.

Babe Ruth was a larger-than-life figure whose baseball accomplishments alone would have elevated him to hero status. But Ruth's on- and off-field behavior kept him in the headlines almost daily. Ruth was also a savvy self-promoter who spent wads of his money courting the press so he would be presented in the best possible light. In the third game of the World Series against the Cubs in 1932, Ruth's home run became known as the "called shot." A frustrated Cubs bench had been razzing Ruth throughout the game. That hostility was picked up by the fans, who screamed at Ruth when he stepped up to the plate. An irate Ruth reacted to two thrown strikes with two fingers in the air. The next pitch he belted for a home run, and as he ran the bases Ruth gestured in victory at the Cubs' bench. Joe Williams, reporter for the *New York World Telegram*, reported, "Ruth pointed to center and punched a screaming liner to a spot where no ball had been hit before." Other reporters picked up on the story and the legend was made. Ruth never denied the story and in subsequent retellings and movies the home run has grown in impressiveness. The "called shot" is just one of the myths that surround Ruth.

Even his teammates perpetuated Ruth's legend. Joe Dugan, Ruth's teammate from 1922 to 1928, stated, "When you figure the things he did, and the way he lived and the way he played, you've got to figure he was more than an animal even. There was never anyone like him. He was a god." This quote appears in the official Yankee retrospective that was published to celebrate the 100th anniversary of the team. Yankee literature such as this official retrospective keeps alive the team legends and their accomplishments. Many years after Ruth's death, he is still the benchmark for superior accomplishment.

His single season home run mark has been eclipsed several times, but no one will ever match his presence and effect on the game. Writers even invented a word for him: Ruthian. Successful organizations need to document the Ruthian accomplishments of their own superstars.

Except for the largest corporations with big tales to relate, few businesses see their stories in print, but they can create a historical record of accomplishments. A business writer or public relations person can be contracted to write your company story and/or an employee can be designated as company librarian. Every company has founding fathers and early pioneers with stories worth repeating and embellishing. Every company has noteworthy events that can be enhanced in writing. Write the best stories you can tell. The stories can be combined into an annual accounting of company success. This book can be distributed to all employees and potential hires, as well as to current and potential clients. Written histories are statements of company pride. They announce that you have a story worthy of documentation, and all associated with the organization can feel proud of being part of that story.

Exploit the Charisma of Colorful People

Yogi Berra had a Hall of Fame career that spanned the years from 1946 to 1963 as catcher with the Yankees, one year playing for the Mets, Yankee manager during two different eras, and Mets manager. Berra can qualify as one of the best catchers of all time. He appeared in a record 14 World Series. He holds the record for most Series games and most Series hits. He is also the only catcher to call a perfect World Series game. He won three Most Valuable Player awards in the 1950s and was beaten out for a fourth honor by his teammate Phil Rizzuto during Berra's most statistically impressive season.

But Berra's statistics are less quoted than his "Yogi-isms," which have made him the most quoted man in all of sports. He has promoted his unique way of looking at the world through the publication of several books, including *The Yogi Book: "I Really Didn't Say Everything I Said"*; *When You Come to a Fork in the Road, Take It!: Inspiration and Wisdom from One of Baseball's Greatest Heroes*; and *What Time Is It? You Mean Now?: Advice for Life from the Zennest Master of Them All.* These titles and the books' Yogi-isms boost Berra's legendary image.

Casey Stengel is another Yankees legend who camouflaged his baseball intelligence with colorful language that came to be known as Stengelese. He, too, promoted himself through publication of a book, *Quotable Casey: The Wit, Wisdom, and Wacky World of Casey Stengel, Baseball's Old Perfessor and Most Amazing Manager.* Both Stengel and Berra have become Yankee legends through their own words and accomplishments and the words of many others who have written about these two unique individuals.

Take advantage of the unique and colorful people in your company. Every company has someone who stands out for some skill beyond work accomplishments. Do you have a person who has an area of niche expertise or outstanding skill or an individual who stands out for athletic accomplishment? Make these people company ambassadors. Showcase their skills in-house and in the community. There are numerous ways for creating a company legend and developing organization goodwill at the same time through selected exposure of your special people. You can host a pre- or postwork employee get-together featuring your unique talents as speakers or demonstrators. The community is a large arena for special events featuring your employees. People appreciate opportunities to showcase their special skills, and most would welcome their company recognizing and sponsoring them. Utilize your employees to create organization legends beyond work accomplishments. Berra's and Stengel's baseball accomplishments made them superstars, but their unique personas established them as legends. Your organization can enhance your folklore around your special people.

Make Reunions (Old Timers Day) a Regular Event

The Yankees take Old Timers Day seriously. It is an annual event when Yankee superstars of the past visit the Stadium and participate in a special intramural game. Sometimes the game is played between former Yankee players and other times it is played with retired players from other teams. It's a popular fan-attracting event with a larger purpose. It provides an opportunity for current players to meet and talk with Yankees of old, but it also exposes current Yankee fans to the legends and traditions of yesterday. History comes alive when a retired superstar steps on the field. Current players have an opportunity to rub shoulders and to observe the habits and jargon of past Yankees. The key attitudes, especially concerning winning, that have made the Yankees a dynasty are conveyed to a new generation.

Many companies recognize the importance of bringing back alumni/ae to share stories with the current group of employees. Any organization can establish an annual alumni/ae event where past employees can be welcomed back as speakers or just to mingle with current employees. It is a perfect opportunity to perpetuate company anecdotes down to a new generation.

Provide a Formal Event to Recognize Fan Appreciation

Baseball teams usually celebrate Fan Appreciation Day on the final day of the official baseball season. The Yankees take part in this tradition. In addition to distributing some special thank-you such as a team photo, the team uses the day to showcase the season's memorable moments. Between innings, outstanding player feats are flashed on a large screen. The team is imprinting its best accomplishments in the minds of fans often to be discussed and rehashed during the off-season as baseball fans are apt to do. Baseball folklore can be created as fans tell and retell magic moments.

Every organization should recognize that its fan base (customers) can help it create, and share, company folklore when it holds a Fan Appreciation Day. Customers are invited to a special day where they receive tokens of appreciation, such as a sample of a new product or even a book detailing company accomplishments. Over refreshments company achievements can be highlighted while thanks are extended to customers for making these achievements possible. Customers can be a source of company lore when they tell others about their special experiences with your company.

Use Spring Training to Inculcate Players with the Tools for Success

The tradition of winning is transferred every year to new players during spring training. The Yankees frequently bring their most technically competent former players, who also exemplify the four classes of Yankee competencies, to help the current players improve their skills and learn the Yankee Way. During this annual training and development event, champions of the past testify to the rewards for following the tenets of the team. The former players appreciate the opportunity to stay involved, and emerging talents appreciate learning directly from their heroes.

Your company should utilize former or retired employees to teach professional skills to emerging talent. These former employees know firsthand your company's competencies and values. As in spring training, this is a win-win situation for former and current employees.

Hire Former Players as Coaches and Managers

Appointing former Yankee players to coaching positions on the parent team and front-office jobs in the farm system is another way the Yankees perpetuate their tradition. These former players are selected because they exemplify the Yankee image and can convey in both verbal and nonverbal ways the values of the organization. Yankee heroes continue to contribute to Yankee winning long after their playing days. In the 2004 season most of the Yankee coaching staff was composed of former players. Among them Don Mattingly, former captain, was batting coach; Roy White, outfielder from 1965 to 1979, was first base coach; and Mel Stottlemyre, pitching standout from 1964 to 1974, was pitching coach. Coaches impart their knowledge of the game and Yankee tradition on a daily basis.

As your star employees age and spend many years in the same position, they may be blocking the movement of an emerging talent into that position. Your company should consider using these still contributing and vital employees in coaching and mentoring capacities. They can pass on your company wisdom and traditions while instructing in professional skills and opening their current position to a backup. You can also consider bringing retired superstars and stars out of retirement on a part-time basis to mentor and coach.

Use the Press to Promote Your Organization's Mystique

The Yankees are fortunate to be located in New York, which in itself carries a mystique for people in and outside of the city. Everything in New York appears larger and brassier than elsewhere. The Yankees are the right team for such a flashy city. The Yankees maintain an image of conceit and aggressiveness that fits the city image. The New York sportswriters, most of whom also are representative of the city in which they work, do their part in sustaining and creating Yankee mythology. Provocative news sells newspapers and magazines. The Yankees' real or imagined events magnified by the sportswriters provide stimulating press. In the 1970s, "notes and quotes" columns based on juicy baseball tidbits started appearing in the Sunday newspapers. Dick Young of the *New York Daily News* wrote "Clubhouse Confidential"; these articles became as popular as the Broadway gossip columns. When Young wrote about what attracted Reggie Jackson to sign with the Yankees, he noted, "While George [Steinbrenner]'s competition was offering nothing more than filthy lucre, George offered filthy New York—beautiful, big, bustling, exciting, pressurized, hurrying, unfunctioning, sexy, cultured, glamorous, filthy New York." Gossip-hungry fans prized these columns.

Your organization may not be located in a city as scintillating as New York, and your company may not be as provocative news as the Yankees, but you can utilize the press to your advantage. Assign a company spokesperson to court the local press. This can be as simple as weekly telephone calls mingling networking with organization accomplishments. Have the same person develop ongoing press releases that note company tidbits such as new hires, promotions, and so on. Like the Yankee front office leaks stories to be picked up by the media, your company, too, can disclose tidbits that will develop the aura that you wish to create.

Highlight Awards and Honors That Reinforce the Yankee Way

Major League Baseball has established many avenues for rewarding and honoring its superstars. The annual announcement of these awards is anxiously anticipated by the baseball world, and the recipients are forever enshrined in baseball history. Yankee players have received a hefty share of these awards, and they become part of the Yankee folklore and serve as incentives to emerging talent. They are coveted and stand as benchmarks for the best of the best.

The most esteemed award in Major League Baseball is to be elected to the National Baseball Hall of Fame. Election to the Hall of Fame ensures perpetual inclusion in an exclusive club that automatically grants legendary status. Since 1936, over 250 men have been inducted into the Hall of Fame, mostly players but also baseball pioneers or executives, managers, and umpires. People from all over the world visit the Baseball Hall of Fame in Cooperstown, New York, to view the baseball history preserved there. The Yankees have 25 Hall of Fame honorees; almost 10 percent of the total. These not only include their legendary players but also managers and front office pioneers like Ed Barrow and George Weiss. For the Yankees, and any franchise, having members in the Hall of Fame is an endless source of pride and bragging rights. Yankee folklore is enshrined on hallowed ground outside of Yankee Stadium.

Baseball is replete with annual honors. The Most Valuable Player (MVP) in each league is chosen by the Baseball Writers' Association of America. This award is an enormous feather in the cap of the players so honored, and the Yankees have received their just desserts in this category. Babe Ruth was named MVP once, Lou Gehrig twice, Joe DiMaggio three times, Yogi Berra three times, Mickey Mantle three times, and Roger Maris twice. In all, from 1923 to 1985, Yankee players have garnered MVP honors 20 times, a most dynastic achievement.

The Cy Young award is presented annually by the Baseball Writers' Association of America to the most outstanding pitcher in each league. Again, the Yankees have augmented their history with five Cy Young winners, including most recently Roger Clemens in 2001. The Gold Glove award honors those with outstanding fielding. Again, the Yankees have been well represented in this category. There is even a Rookie of the Year honor, presented to the most outstanding emerging superstar in each league. Most recently for the Yankees Derek Jeter earned this distinction in 1996. There are many additional annual awards for on- and off-field accomplishments. Each award adds its own mystique to the aura of superstar players.

Most organizations are not in industries that have nationally visible honors and distinctions. However, every industry has its annual conventions, banquets, and meetings where awards are bestowed on its outstanding people. Within the industry, these awards are as coveted and revered as the baseball awards. Every organization should discover the awards in its industry and make it a company policy to nominate employees for these awards. When employees are honored at conventions and other public occasions, a company should send not only top executives to view the granting of the award but also emerging talent who can be inspired to work for these distinctions. The company should have in-house acknowledgment of these awards with visible plaques naming the award and the recipient. Again, this is another way of recognizing outstanding achievers, gaining industry recognition to attract other talent, and establishing your company folklore.

All company awards and honors with biographical sketches of the recipients should be documented in interoffice memos, company literature, and other in-house distribution channels. Even the smallest organization should establish a close relationship to local newspapers to share news of employee recognition.

LESSONS FOR YOUR TEAM

How to implement the "Celebrate Your History, Heroes, and Legends: Creating Traditions of Excellence" principle:

1. Take pride in your organization's past. Every organization has its unique history, values, and skills. Your company's owners, top executives, managers, and superstars are transmitters of your company "way."

2. Document your company's history and traditions in reading materials that are distributed to employees, potential hires, and customers. Literature establishes credibility for a company's worth and perpetuates its folklore.

3. Use your employees' accomplishments both at work and in the community to promote the employees and, through established goodwill, your organization.

4. Establish relationships with the local press. Send a steady stream of press releases announcing company accomplishments, new hires, and promotions to the local newspapers.

5. Hold annual alumni/ae days inviting former employees to both informally and formally speak with current employees. These days are great ways to honor past heroes and successes.

6. Hold customer appreciation events where your company's employees, products, and services are celebrated.

7. Use former employees who are technically competent and who represent company values in formal training and development programs.

8. Use former superstars and stars who embody your company's competencies as mentors and coaches.

9. Solicit industry awards for employee accomplishments. Establish in-house awards to recognize many levels of achievement.
Celebrate your employees' successes.

CHAPTER

14

Boldly Promote Your Tradition of Excellence

The baseball universe expects the New York Yankees to be World Champions every year. Each season brings an expectation that this dynasty will endure. The Yankees have done an incredible job of promoting this winning tradition to all members of the organization, from batboy to players to management to fans and the media. The Yankees began with two organizational promotional goals: associating the Yankee brand with winning, and becoming an employer of choice. They accomplish these goals using a four-step strategy: focus on team accomplishments; focus on the superstar; pick colorful and committed hucksters to spread your message; and package the team image in a classical and epic-evoking environment. The Yankee brand was built using these four strategies, and the organization has become one of the most recognizable in the world. People associate the Yankees with winning.

When Americans visit Europe, Asia, and Latin America they frequently encounter people wearing Yankee baseball caps. While it is unlikely that foreigners would accept remuneration to wear an American flag on an article of clothing, they willingly pay for the privilege of wearing a Yankee logo on their caps. When asked why they choose to wear a Yankee cap, these nascent Yankee fans reply that it signifies winning, prestige, and power. The Yankee pinstripes and logo have become universally identified symbols for success.

The power of the Yankee franchise is felt throughout the United States and throughout the world. In 2004, *Sports Illustrated*'s 50th anniversary issues contained state-by-state sports interest polls. Almost every state's survey had the Yankees on the top of its list as a favorite baseball team and/or the biggest rivalry with the local teams of that state. It has taken more than 80 years to build a global identity for winning that is recognized in places as diverse as Japan, Norway, Venezuela, and Montana.

Winning alone does not account for the Yankees' global brand identity. Yankee self-promotion is a major contributing factor. Bob Fishel's role in Yankee promotional activities for a substantial period of time and his broad experience as an executive in Major League Baseball provided insight on the Yankee success at self-promotion. Based on conversations with Fishel, additional discussions with other baseball executives, and subsequent research, it appears that the various teams in the dynasty shared two simple promotional goals and four strategies to achieve these goals. Let's first look at these two goals, and then at the strategies in depth.

Two Promotional Goals: Branding and Employer of Choice

Branding the Yankee franchise so that the team name and logo are associated with preeminence in the sports industry is the primary goal of Yankee management. The Yankee public relations department aims to build a high level of awareness of the Yankees with the players, fans, general public, and media as a championship organization and, therefore, a strong and compelling brand with charisma and mystique—one that people can identify with and be loyal to because of its association with a special way of winning. The Yankee winning way embraces professionalism, citizenship, and leadership as well as accomplishments. This branding helps sell tickets and merchandise, increases viewership, and leads to greater advertising revenues. It also increases "share of audience mind" with respect to its baseball and nonbaseball competitors.

The Yankees' second promotional goal is to establish the team as the indisputable employer of choice. As an employer of choice, the team has a better chance of attracting and retaining quality talent than its competitors. The Yankees convey the message to potential players that their team is where you come to win championships. They accomplish this by clearly conveying the message that ownership is committed to helping the team sustain success by investing in the resources necessary to complete the journey. It becomes clear to prospective players that even superstars do not have to carry the team by themselves. The Yankees will procure other players capable of contributing to success. Even before players join the team, the Yankees promote to them the elitist conviction that only special players wear the Yankee pinstripes. Most ballplayers aspire to be Yankees and once they are Yankees desire to stay Yankees for their whole careers.

These are the two main goals of promotion. Every organization wants to be branded as a winner and known as an employer of choice, but accomplishing those two lofty goals takes masterful strategic management. Let's look at how the Yankees are able to accomplish this feat.

Four Promotional Strategies to Sustain Success

The Yankees use four promotional strategies to achieve their goals. They are:

1. Focus on team accomplishments.

2. Focus on the superstar.

3. Pick colorful and committed hucksters to spread their message.

4. Package the team image in a classical and epic-evoking environment.

Focus on Team Accomplishments

The Yankees have established a clear and simple message emphasizing the team's winning tradition, high standards, professionalism, citizenship, and leadership. The message is communicated consistently through every communication channel. The message includes basic facts of Yankee existence. The primary promotional point is the Yankees are number one. By wearing a cap or jacket with the Yankee logo, the wearer associates himself or herself with more than an individual player; the wearer is connected with a rich tradition of winning teams.

One of the unique ways the Yankees promote the concept of team is by creating intergenerational competition. This means that Yankee players, fans, and media frequently compare a team with different Yankee teams within the dynasty rather than with non-Yankee teams. Was the 1998 team better than the 1961 team? Was the 1927 team the best Yankee team of all time? Countless time is spent by the team, fans, and media analyzing and discussing the accomplishments and qualities of each winning team, what made them successful and why. These discussions augment the Yankee mystique by converting historical facts into folklore. These public forums elaborate on the ingredients of success from a team perspective while simultaneously creating a healthy environment of mythic competition. The latter makes old-timers games more interesting as history come alive for everyone.

Every manager and organization can promote the accomplishments of their own team or unit. They can compare themselves with past and present units; and they can promote their unit's excellence to their bosses and to outsiders. They can cite accomplishments and establish why the group operates successfully. Like the Yankees, they can have special days to invite back members of successful past organizations to discuss why they were great and how they compare with today's organization. Regular nostalgia events will encourage a dialogue of excellence and imprint past successes in the minds of current employees. A healthy discussion could be sparked for current employees to best the tales of their unit's achievements.

Focus on the Superstar

Communicating colossal and momentous tales of superstar heroics is effective in communicating an organization's values, beliefs, and competencies. The world is a stage and superstars are the lead actors! People love to associate with winners, live vicariously through their accomplishments, be present at events honoring them, and hope to ingest some secrets to becoming a winner.

For the Yankees, the focus is on superstars operating the Yankee Way. There are countless examples of the Yankees capitalizing on the accomplishments of their superstars. What could be more epic than Babe Ruth's 60 home runs? He broke his own record of 59 and set the standard of comparison for all future sluggers. His batting prowess coined the adjective "Ruthian," which would be a source of inspiration for heroic deeds of others who would succeed him. Lou Gehrig's incredible consecutive games played record would become a tribute to all people whose work attendance is exemplary and who have the perseverance, drive, and organizational loyalty to show up and produce every day. The term "Iron Horse" was coined to describe Gehrig. Joe DiMaggio's 52-game hitting streak was a testament to hard work and productivity under stress. Mickey Mantle's great accomplishments under great physical duress make him a role model for handling adversity and hardship. Yogi Berra, despite the fact that he was considered too short and awkward to ever make it to the big leagues, became a superstar and Hall of Fame honoree. These are but a few examples that spotlight superstar achievements as a metaphor for success the Yankee Way. Each superstar's feats are reflective of high levels of accomplishment achieved through evidencing the core values of the team. All of these feats and accomplishments are represented in the Yankee brand.

Pick Colorful and Committed Hucksters to Spread Your Message

Organization cheerleaders elevate the perception of the company by serving as candid, positive voices for the organization's accomplishments and values. They inspire both those inside and outside the organization. We call these cheerleaders "hucksters." Every organization needs its hucksters. They are the true believers in the organization and what it stands for. They inspire others to want to be part of the organization or associate with it.

The Yankee hucksters have included owners, professional broad-cast announcers, current and former players, an organist, the field an-nouncer, the clubhouse manager, and even a popular singer. Because of their visibility and upbeat demeanor, many hucksters become as legendary as some of the principal owners, managers, and superstars. The hucksters have two critical aspects in common: They love the team, and they embrace its values. Among the myriad of team huck-sters, four stand out as contributing significantly to the Yankee mys-tique. They are Yankee legends in their own right. We selected them because of their obvious success at Yankee promotion and because their role can be duplicated in other organizations. Let's look at each of these in depth.

Mel Allen: The Voice of the Yankees

Mel Allen was the Yankee broadcaster and chief huckster from 1939 through 1964. He was also a team historian who bridged the 25 years of tradition from Ruth to Mantle. Allen was present when Gehrig and Ruth said their farewells, for Roger Maris' 61st home run, and for almost all of Mantle's prodigious home runs. He was dubbed the "Voice of the Yankees" and his persona became almost indistinguishable from that of the team. Allen may have been the team's greatest fan, and it appeared that he embodied many of the same qualities as the team's managers and players. He had a com-prehensive knowledge of the game and its rules, he was meticulous in his broadcast preparation, and he supported the team values. He was a positive influence on the players and his pleasant Southern style was disarming.

Allen coined many phrases that became associated with the Yankee image. For example, his reaction to a great accomplishment on the field was "How about that!" He also linked sponsors' prod-ucts to the Yankee accomplishments by referring to home runs as

"Ballantine blasts." Idioms like this became part of the Yankee folk-lore and further disseminated the Yankee brand of excellence. Fans and nonfans alike picked up Allen's colorful descriptions.

Mel Allen, like the Yankees, was a champion. He won the Ford C. Frick award, Major League Baseball's decoration for preeminent skills in broadcasting, and was elected to the National Sportscasters Hall of Fame. Allen was the personification of the Yankees to many fans. To the chagrin of fans and colleagues, Allen was unceremoni-ously dismissed after the 1964 season for unknown reasons. The "Voice of the Yankees" was silenced. This event was not befitting the Yankee image—there was no grace or respect in the act. The dismissal brought bad publicity to the team and it turned out to be a bad omen. It presaged the CBS dark age, when the Yankees not only went with-out championships but went without playing in the postseason at all. It came at a time when Yankee stars were aging, the farm system was eroding, and there was an absence of a principal owner. Allen was a peerless promoter of the team, and when he was gone the fabric of the dynasty seemed to come apart.

Allen, like Ruth, Gehrig, DiMaggio, and Mantle, is a Yankee folk hero whose spirit is indelibly ingrained in the team's mystique. In many organizations, Allen would be the person serving as the public face to the customers, shareholders, and media. In reality, any member of an organizational unit or team who can speak in a convincing way about his or her company and colleagues could ful-fill Allen's role.

BOB SHEPPARD: THE "VOICE OF GOD"

While Mel Allen was named the "Voice of the Yankees," Bob Shep-pard, the public address announcer at Yankee Stadium, was dubbed the "Voice of God." He earned this title because of his booming yet thoughtful way of announcing players and key activities at the stadium. To many people, Sheppard's voice sounded almost biblical or, at least, epical. Like Mel Allen he embodied the values of the Yankee team. He had a record of professional accomplishment reflected in his previous role as a speech professor, his impeccable technical speaking skills, his exemplary personal life, and his love of the Yankees.

Sheppard started with the Yankees in 1951, and from the beginning added his own unique style that enhanced the Yankee images of excellence and formidability. Like Allen, his tenure transcended those of the players he announced. Sheppard defined his role as a unique presenter of player and stadium activities. His voice came to be associated with Yankee success.

In the corporate world Sheppard could be any cheerleader who uniquely presents the organization's accomplishments and exhibits a strong interest in promoting team activity. These people should be encouraged in their booster efforts through company acknowledgment and awards.

PETE SHEEHY: THE VOICE OF EVERYMAN

Pete Sheehy was the Yankee clubhouse attendant from 1927 to 1985. Pete was the unofficial "Voice of Everyman." It is important for people like Pete to have a favorable opinion of their work environment because they speak to a large group of outside constituents who in turn speak to an even larger group of constituents. The circles emanating from workers like Pete keep expanding ad infinitum. Like Mel Allen and Bob Sheppard, Pete embodied Yankee strengths, values, and beliefs. He was diligent, self-sacrificing, and loyal. It was rumored that Billy Martin, in a fit of despair, once asked Sheehy to pull the day's lineup out of cards in a hat. This is a sardonic example of management inviting a worker to participate in the decision-making process. Sheehy's lineup resulted in an improved record and the media applauded his "choice."

Sheehy was an important spokesperson for the team because he knew its most intimate secrets. Sheehy's words had great impact because every fan could relate to him. Whatever the reality, Sheehy put a good spin on everything. His first priority was preserving the Yankee image when speaking with outsiders. Members of the press seeking to gain insight into the behaviors of team members occasionally interviewed Sheehy. One reporter, seeking to gain the inside scoop on Babe Ruth, tried to get Sheehy to speak negatively of Ruth. Sheehy responded by conceding that the worst thing about Ruth was that "he did not flush the toilet."

Sheehy also played a critical role in perpetuating Yankee mystique through his actions around the clubhouse. He placed a quote from Joe DiMaggio behind the door of the clubhouse. It read, "I want to thank the Good Lord for making me a Yankee." The words echoed Sheehy's feelings about his job. On a conspicuous place in a tunnel leading to the field Sheehy placed a quote from General Douglas MacArthur that stated, "There is no substitute for victory."

Every employee is the voice of your organization. Reporters will probably not be seeking interviews with your employees to get the inside scoop on your company, unlike Sheehy on the Yankees, but every employee has a life outside the job. People speak to other people about their work experiences and work environment, and those people in turn will relate good stories to others. Your organization's people are an excellent public relations vehicle. Satisfied employees are your best means for achieving employer of choice status.

EDDIE LAYTON: THE SOUND OF THE YANKEES

If Mel Allen, Bob Sheppard, and Pete Sheehy were voices of the Yankees, legendary organist Eddie Layton was the "Sound of the Yankees." At every home game from 1967 through 2003 Eddie Layton played the organ at Yankee Stadium. He had a longer consecutive game streak than Lou Gehrig. Layton was a model of resoluteness and team loyalty. But Layton's skills went way beyond playing "The Star-Spangled Banner," "Take Me Out to the Ball Game," and a host of rallying cries. He has countless CDs to his credit, represented the Hammond Organ Company, and has played the great Wurlitzer at Radio City Music Hall. Layton represented the team well in many venues by his accomplishments, professionalism, citizenship, and leadership. He once stated, "The fans cheer with their vocal cords, but I cheer with my music." For 18 years Layton played the organ for the New York Rangers and Knicks as well as the Yankees. Like the Yankees on the field, Layton was a winner in his profession.

PRINCIPAL OWNERS: THE HUCKSTER AT THE TOP

Periodically, the principal owners have been hucksters for the team. Mostly their public utterances and behaviors have been limited to acknowledging epic events like the signing of a superstar, or discussing major accomplishments like the winning of a championship. In general, they attempted to comport themselves within the team's image of excellence, strength, pride, and dignity. Except for George Steinbrenner, they were visible but not flamboyant.

Ruppert, Topping, and Webb occasionally stood in the public spotlight and spoke for their team, but they usually let Yankee accomplishments dominate the stage and allowed others to tout the team. Periodically they slipped and made headlines for a controversial statement. However, George Steinbrenner reshaped the owner's role as chief huckster when he took over the team and assumed a far more perceptible role in raising the team's, and his own, visibility. Steinbrenner's tenure began after the CBS dark age, when the team's image was greatly diminished and the Yankees were generating little fan or media attention. Steinbrenner arrived on the scene with the image of a winner. His outward confidence in his ability to make the team successful once again put the Yankees back on the front of the sports pages. His magnified involvement with the team and the media wildly achieved the team's goal of increased public awareness. Initially, this strategy succeeded in increasing the interest of the public and attracting new players. However, Steinbrenner's antics sometimes became a distraction that diverted media attention away from the traditional Yankee Way toward the acrimonious soap opera being played out by ownership and management.

Over time and with the reemergence of the Yankees as a winning team, Steinbrenner has tempered his involvement in controlling every aspect of team management. However, he remains the Yankees' most visible and confident huckster. Steinbrenner regularly appears in television commercials that often parody him, but always keep the Yankees in the public eye.

Package the Team Image in a Classical and Epic-Evoking Environment

From its inception as the "House that Ruth Built," Yankee Stadium took on the mystique of not just another arena, but a magical place. It was the intention of Jacob Ruppert to build it to be mammoth and reverential. Yankee Stadium, with an eventual capacity of more than 70,000, was nearly twice the size of any other park at the time it was built, a time when baseball teams derived most of their revenues from ticket sales. The Stadium provided the Yankees with a source of income unmatched by any other team. Yankee Stadium was the first modern ballpark built for the evolving power and offensive transformation. It was no coincidence that the Yankees won their first championship in their first year in Yankee Stadium, and the Stadium is the only constant in every succeeding championship won by the team.

Yankee Stadium became part of Yankee history and folklore. It is where players learn from the successes of the past and are duty-bound to repeat them. Although Yankee Stadium was refurbished in 1976, its original dimensions are discernible to the fans. A facade-type structure that originally hung from the top of the third deck was moved to the top of the center field bleachers, where it evokes memories of Mickey Mantle almost hitting the only fair ball out of Yankee Stadium—twice.

Monument Park contains the retired uniform numbers, plaques, and monuments of the Yankee legends. In addition to players, Monument Park memorializes Jacob Ruppert and Ed Barrow, founders of the Yankee dynasty, and Mel Allen and Bob Sheppard, the two voices of the Yankees. Fans coming to Yankee Stadium seek out Monument Park to immerse themselves in Yankee tradition. The most visible piece of Yankee folklore, beyond the Stadium itself, is the 120-foot high replica of Babe Ruth's bat just outside an entrance gate that has been named after Pete Sheehy.

Every organization, big or small, can affect its physical surroundings in such a way as to celebrate its successes and successful people. Yankee Stadium stands as a symbol of a physical environment that incubates success. Any manager can build his or her own version of Yankee Stadium by shaping work areas to include recognized symbols of organizational and individual triumphs. Distinctive areas that contain memorabilia such as photos and awards placed in clear view of outsiders and insiders shouts out the message that your organization celebrates accomplishments. Employees who soak up the symbolic lessons of success will be compelled to repeat them.

LESSONS FOR YOUR TEAM

How to implement the "Boldly Promote Your Tradition of Excellence" principle:

1. Help your organization become an employer of choice by ensuring that all employees feel valued and their contributions to organizational success are acknowledged.

2. Know what you are promoting: your organization's goals, values, competencies, and accomplishments.

3. Promote your company's and employees' accomplishments.

4. Promote the heroic accomplishments of superstars internally and externally.

5. Identify, encourage, and turn loose your best hucksters to shout your company's message and accomplishments.

6. Shape your facility so that it exudes your organization's history and accomplishments.

Conclusion

The sustained success of the Yankees is not simply explained by luck or wild spending, although both have affected the evolution of the dynasty. Nor are the conditions that have buttressed Yankee accomplishments solely cloaked in myth and folklore. An analysis of Yankee history and traditions provides us with many probable answers to Yankee success. In this book, Yankee dynastic success is explained by a simple formula consisting of three factors that can be further differentiated into 14 principles. The three factors—leadership, processes, and culture—had their roots in the Yankee organization that launched the dynasty, while the 14 principles evolved over the team's 80-plus-year successful history.

We believe that any organization can achieve Yankee-like success and compete with top rivals without spending colossal amounts of money if it utilizes the three-factor formula more effectively and efficiently than its competitors. This is not an easy task, but if you create the success factors in your organization, you have a good chance of giving rise to a dynasty. Where do you begin?

- First, you must establish a strong and pervasive leadership structure, beginning with a principal owner who can credibly influence employees to achieve a clearly defined goal for competitive success.

- Second, the organizational goal of the leaders must be translated into a road map comprised of a set of credible, clear, and practical processes the organization must follow to reach its goal. Perhaps the two critical processes are (1) the talent evaluation system consisting of well-defined selection criteria and superior talent recruiters and assessors and (2) an organization-wide talent development system that provides a steady stream of high-quality replacements.

- Third, there must be a conscious effort by leaders to create and sustain a culture where employees are motivated to establish personal goals that derive value from their contribution to organizational success.

Once you achieve success you must sustain it to become a dynasty. To paraphrase the great Yogi Berra, you must constantly achieve "déjà vu all over again."

Appendix:
Yankee Championship Teams and Key Player Roles

YEAR	HIGHEST SEASON ACCOMPLISHMENT	MANAGER	SUPERSTARS	KEY POSITION PITCHER	KEY POSITION CATCHER
1921	AL Pennant	Huggins	Hoyt, Ruth	Hoyt (SS) Mays (S) Shawkey (S)	Schang (S)
1922	AL Pennant	Huggins	Hoyt, Ruth	Bush (S) Hoyt (SS) Mays (S) Shawkey (S)	Schang (S)
1923	World Series	Huggins	Hoyt, Pennock, Ruth	Bush (S) Hoyt (SS) Pennock (SS) Shawkey (S)	Schang (S)
1926	AL Pennant	Huggins	Combs, Gehrig, Hoyt, Lazzeri, Pennock, Ruth	Hoyt (SS) Pennock (SS) Shawkey (S) Shocker (S)	
1927	World Series	Huggins	Combs, Gehrig, Hoyt, Lazzeri, Pennock, Ruth	Hoyt (SS) Pennock (SS) Shawkey (S) Shocker (S)	
1928	World Series	Huggins	Combs, Gehrig, Hoyt, Lazzeri, Pennock, Ruth	Hoyt (SS) Pennock (SS) Pipgras (S)	
1932	World Series	McCarthy	Combs, Gehrig, Gomez, Hoyt, Lazzeri, Ruffing, Ruth	Gomez (SS) Pennock (S) Pipgras (S) Ruffing (SS)	Dickey (SS)
1936	World Series	McCarthy	Dickey, DiMaggio, Gehrig, Gomez, Lazzeri, Ruffing	Gomez (SS) Murphy (S) Ruffing (SS)	Dickey (SS)
1937	World Series	McCarthy	Dickey, DiMaggio, Gehrig, Gomez, Lazzeri	Chandler (S) Gomez (SS) Murphy (S) Ruffing (SS)	Dickey (SS)

APPENDIX

YEAR	HIGHEST SEASON ACCOMPLISHMENT	MANAGER	SUPERSTARS	KEY POSITION PITCHER	KEY POSITION CATCHER
1938	World Series	McCarthy	Dickey, DiMaggio, Gehrig, Gomez, Ruffing	Chandler (S) Gomez (SS) Murphy (S) Ruffing (SS)	Dickey (SS)
1939	World Series	McCarthy	Dickey, DiMaggio, Gomez, Ruffing	Chandler (S) Gomez (SS) Ruffing (SS)	Dickey (SS)
1941	World Series	McCarthy	Dickey, DiMaggio, Rizzuto, Ruffing	Chandler (S) Gomez (SS) Ruffing (SS)	Dickey (SS)
1942	AL Pennant	McCarthy	Dickey, DiMaggio, Rizzuto, Ruffing	Chandler (S) Gomez (SS) Murphy (S) Ruffing (SS)	Dickey (SS)
1943	World Series	McCarthy	Dickey	Chandler (S) Murphy (S)	Dickey (SS)
1947	World Series	Harris	DiMaggio, Rizzuto	Chandler (S) Page (S) Raschi (S) Reynolds (S)	
1949	World Series	Stengel	Berra, DiMaggio, Rizzuto	Lopat (S) Page (S) Raschi (S) Reynolds (S)	Berra (SS)
1950	World Series	Stengel	Berra, DiMaggio, Ford, Rizzuto	Ford (SS) Lopat (S) Page (S) Raschi (S) Reynolds (S)	Berra (SS)
1951	World Series	Stengel	Berra, DiMaggio, Rizzuto	Lopat (S) Raschi (S) Reynolds (S)	Berra (SS)
1952	World Series	Stengel	Berra, Mantle, Rizzuto	Lopat (S) Raschi (S) Reynolds (S)	Berra (SS)
1953	World Series	Stengel	Berra, Ford, Mantle, Rizzuto	Ford (SS) Lopat (S) Raschi (S) Reynolds (S)	Berra (SS)
1955	AL Pennant	Stengel	Berra, Ford, Mantle, Rizzuto	Ford (SS) Turley (S)	Berra (SS)
1956	World Series	Stengel	Berra, Ford, Mantle, Rizzuto	Ford (SS) Turley (S)	Berra (SS)
1957	AL Pennant	Stengel	Berra, Ford, Mantle	Ford (SS) Turley (S)	Berra (SS)

YEAR	HIGHEST SEASON ACCOMPLISHMENT	MANAGER	SUPERSTARS	KEY POSITION PITCHER	KEY POSITION CATCHER
1958	World Series	Stengel	Berra, Ford, Mantle	Ford (SS) Turley (S)	Berra (SS)
1960	AL Pennant	Stengel	Berra, Ford, Mantle	Ford (SS) Terry (S) Turley (S)	Berra (SS)
1961	World Series	Houk	Berra, Ford, Mantle	Ford (SS) Terry (S) Turley (S)	Berra (SS)
1962	World Series	Houk	Berra, Ford, Mantle	Ford (SS) Terry (S)	Berra (SS) Howard (S)
1963	AL Pennant	Houk	Ford, Mantle	Ford (SS) Terry (S)	Howard (S)
1964	AL Pennant	Berra	Ford, Mantle	Ford (SS) Terry (S)	Howard (S)
1976	AL Pennant	Martin	Hunter	Figueroa (S) Hunter (SS) Lyle (S)	Munson (S)
1977	World Series	Martin	Hunter, Jackson	Figueroa (S) Guidry (S) Hunter (SS) Lyle (S)	Munson (S)
1978	World Series	Martin, Lemon	Hunter, Jackson	Figueroa (S) Gossage (S) Guidry (S) Hunter (SS) Lyle (S)	Munson (S)
1980	ALDS	Howser	Jackson	Gossage (S) Guidry (S) John (S)	
1981	ALCS	Michael, Lemon	Jackson	Gossage (S) Guidry (S) John (S)	
1995	AL Wild Card	Showalter	Rivera*	Cone (S) Pettitte (S) Rivera (SS)* Wetteland (S)	
1996	World Series	Torre	Jeter*, Rivera*	Cone (S) Pettitte (S) Rivera (SS)* Wetteland (S)	Posada (S)
1997	AL Wild Card	Torre	Jeter*, Rivera*	Cone (S) Pettitte (S) Rivera (SS)* Wells (S)	Posada (S)

APPENDIX

YEAR	HIGHEST SEASON ACCOMPLISHMENT	MANAGER	SUPERSTARS	KEY POSITION PITCHER	KEY POSITION CATCHER
1998	World Series	Torre	Jeter*, Rivera*	Cone (S) Pettitte (S) Rivera (SS)* Wells (S)	Posada (S)
1999	World Series	Torre	Clemens*, Jeter*, Rivera*	Clemens (SS)* Cone (S) Pettitte (S) Rivera (SS)*	Posada (S)
2000	World Series	Torre	Clemens*, Jeter*, Rivera*	Clemens (SS)* Cone (S) Pettitte (S) Rivera (SS)*	Posada (S)
2001	ALCS	Torre	Clemens*, Jeter*, Rivera*	Clemens (SS)* Mussina (S) Pettitte (S) Rivera (SS)*	Posada (S)
2002	ALDS Champ	Torre	Clemens*, Jeter*, Rivera*	Clemens (SS)* Pettitte (S) Rivera (SS)* Wells (S)	Posada (S)
2003	ALCS	Torre	Clemens*, Jeter*, Rivera*	Clemens (SS)* Mussina (S) Pettitte (S) Rivera (SS)* Wells (S)	Posada (S)
2004	ALDS	Torre	Jeter*, Rivera*	Brown (S) Mussina (S) Rivera (SS)*	Posada (S)

(SS) Superstar.
(S) Star.
*Potential Hall of Fame candidate.

Index